The Heavenly Dispute

Ibn Rajab Al-Hanbali

The Messenger of Allah, peace and blessings be upon him, said:

"...I woke up and lo and behold! I was with my Lord, the Mighty and Majestic, in the best of forms and He said to me: “O Muhammad, what do you think the highest gatherings (of angels) are in dispute about?...”

[Ahmad, Al-Musnad, 5/243]

Contents

Chapter Five (67)

The Mention of *the Ranks* as reported in the Hadith of Muadh (radiyAllahu anhu)

Chapter Six (99)

Mention of the Supplications made in the Hadith

Great Books

Search by **ISBN** to buy the correct book

Stories of the Prophets	ISBN: 9781643543888
The Noble Quran (Arabic)	ISBN: 9781643543994
Koran (English: Easy to Read)	ISBN: 9781643540924
Life in al-Barzakh: Life after Death	ISBN: 9781643544144
Disciplining the Soul	ISBN: 9781643544151
Timeless Seeds of Advice	ISBN: 9781643544069
Diseases of the Hearts & Cures	ISBN 9781643544106
The Path to Guidance	ISBN: 9781643544052
Miracles of the Prophet	ISBN: 9781643544038
Seerah of Prophet Muhammad	ISBN: 9781643543222
Book on Islam and Marriage	ISBN: 9781073877140
Great Women of Islam	ISBN: 9781643543758
Stories of the Koran	ISBN: 9781095900796
The Purification of the Soul	ISBN: 9781643541389
Al-Fawaid: Wise Sayings	ISBN: 9781727812718
The Book of Hajj	ISBN: 9781072243335
40 Hadith Qudsi	ISBN: 9781070655949
40 Hadith Nawawi	ISBN: 9781070547428
The Legacy of the Prophet	ISBN: 9781080249343
The Ideal Muslim Woman	ISBN: 9781643543192
The Soul's Journey after Death	ISBN: 9781643541365
Khalid Bin Al-Waleed	ISBN: 9781643543420
The Islamic View of Jesus	ISBN: 978164354335
Don't Be Sad	ISBN: 9781643543451
Ota Benga	ISBN: 9798698096665

THE AUTHOR

Ḥāfiẓ Abū'l-Faraj ibn Rajab al-Ḥanbalī

His Name and Lineage

He is the Imām and Ḥāfiẓ, Zaynu'l-Dīn 'Abdul-Raḥmān ibn Aḥmad ibn 'Abdul-Raḥmān ibn al-Ḥasan ibn Muḥammad ibn Abū-l-Barakāt Mas'ūd al-Sulamī al-Ḥanbalī al-Dimashqī. His agnomen was Abū'l-Faraj, and his nickname was Ibn Rajab, which was the nickname of his grandfather who was born in month of Rajab.

His Birth and Upbringing

He was born in Baghdād in 736H and was raised in a pious household that was firmly rooted in knowledge, nobility and righteousness. His grandfather, 'Abdul-Raḥmān ibn al-Ḥasan, was one of the scholars of Baghdād who had a circle in which he would teach students ḥadīth using an ancient method for memorisation. Ibn Rajab would attend these lessons of his grandfather on several occasions even though he was just four-five years of age. As for his father, he was also a scholar and *Muḥaddith*, well-known for his knowledge and virtue.

His Teachers

He learned and took knowledge from the greatest scholars of his time. In Damascus, he studied under:

- Ibn Qayyim al-Jawziyyah, studying closely with him until his death in 751H
- Zaynu'l-Dīn al-ʿIrāqī, ibn an-Naqīb
- Muḥammad ibn Ismāʿīl al-Khabbāz
- Dāwūd ibn Ibrāhīm al-ʿAṭṭār
- Ibn Qāṭī al-Jabal
- Aḥmad ibn ʿAbdu-l-Hādī al-Ḥanbalī

In Makkah, he heard from:

- al-Fakhr ʿUthmān ibn Yūsuf al-Nuwayrī

In Jerusalem, he heard from:

- al-Ḥāfiẓ al-ʿAlāʾī

In Egypt, he heard from:

- Ṣadru'l-Dīn Abū'l-Fatḥ al-Maydūmī
- Nāṣiru'l-Dīn ibn al-Mulūk

and many others.

His Students

Many students of knowledge came to him to study under him. Amongst the most famous of his students were:

- Abū'l-ʿAbbās Aḥmad ibn Abū Bakr ibn ʿAlī al-Ḥanbalī, known as Ibn al-Risām [d. 884H]
- Abū'l-Faḍl Aḥmad ibn Naṣr ibn Aḥmad, the *Muftī* of the lands of Egypt [d. 844H]

- Dāwūd ibn Sulaymān al-Mawsilī [d. 844H]
- 'Abdu'l-Raḥmān ibn Aḥmad ibn Muḥammad al-Muqrī'
- Zaynū'l-Dīn 'Abdu'l-Raḥmān ibn Sulaymān ibn Abū'l-Karam, well known as Abū Shi'ar;
- Abū Dharr 'Abdu'l-Raḥmān Ibn Muḥammad al-Miṣrī al-Zarkashī[d. 846H]
- al-Qāḍī 'Alā'ū'l-Dīn ibn al-Lahām al-Ba'lī [d. 803H], who was the closest of his students to him.
- Aḥmad ibn Ṣayfū'l-Dīn al-Ḥamawī
- and many others.

Ibn Rajab devoted himself to knowledge and spent the vast majority of his time researching, writing, authoring, teaching, and giving legal rulings.

The Scholars Praise for Him

Many scholars praised him for his vast knowledge, asceticism and expertise in the Ḥanbalī *madhhab.* Ibn Qāḍī Shuhbah said of him, 'He read and became proficient in the various fields of science. He engrossed himself with the issues of the *madhhab* until he mastered it. He devoted himself to the occupation of knowledge of the texts, defects and meanings of the ḥadīth.'[1]

Ibn Ḥajr said of him, 'He was highly proficient in the science of ḥadīth in terms of the names of reporters, their biographies, their paths of narration and awareness of their meanings.'[2]

Ibn Mufliḥ said of him, 'He is the Shaykh, the great scholar, the

[1] Ibn Qāḍī al-Shuhbah, *Tārīkh*, vol. 3, p. 195.

[2] ibn Ḥajr, *Inbā'u'l-Ghamr*, vol. 1, p. 460.

Ḥāfiẓ, the ascetic and the Shaykh of the Ḥanbalī *madhhab*.'[3]

His Written Works

He authored many beneficial works, some of them were outstanding such as *al-Qawā'id al-Kubrā fi'l-Furū'* about which it was said, 'It is one of the wonders of this age.'[4] His commentary to al-Tirmidhī is said to be the most extensive and best ever written so much so that al-'Irāqī; about whom ibn Ḥajr said, 'He was the wonder of his age'; would ask for his help when compiling his own commentary to the same book.

Moreover he has many valuable monographs explaining various aḥādīth such as:

- *Sharḥ Ḥadīth Mā Dhi'bāni Jāi'ān Ursilā fī Ghanam*;
- *Ikhtiyār al-Awlā Sharḥ Ḥadīth Ikhtiṣām al-Mala' al-A'lā*;
- *Nūr al-Iqtibās fī Sharḥ Waṣiyyah al-Nabī li ibn 'Abbās*;
- *Kashfu'l-Kurbah fī Wasfi Ḥāli Ahli-l-Ghurbah.*
- *al-Dhull wa'l-Inkisār li'l-'Azīz al-Jabbār*, this book has also been published under the title *al-Khushū' fi'l-Ṣalāh.*
- *Ghayāt al-Nafa' fī Sharḥ Ḥadīth Tamthīl ul-Mu'min bi-Khāmat al-Zara'*
- *al-Maḥajjah fī Sayri'l-Dulja*

In exegesis his works include:

- *Tafsīr Sūrah al-Ikhlāṣ*;
- *Tafsīr Sūrah al-Fātiḥah*;
- *Tafsīr Sūrah al-Naṣr*;
- *I'rāb al-Basmalah*

---

[3] *al-Maqṣad al-Arshad*, vol. 2, p. 81.

[4] ibn 'Abdu'l-Hādī, *Dhayl 'alā Ṭabaqāt ibn Rajab*, p. 38.

- *al-Istighnā' bi'l-Qur'ān.*

In ḥadīth his works include:

- *Sharḥ Jāmi' al-Tirmidhī*
- *Fatḥu'l-Bārī Sharḥ Ṣaḥīḥ al-Bukhārī*
- *Jāmi' al-'Ulūm wa'l-Ḥikam*

In *fiqh* his works include:

- *al-Istikhrāj fī Aḥkām al-Kharāj;*
- *al-Qawā'id al-Fiqhiyyah.*

In biographies his works include:

- The monumental *Dhayl 'alā Ṭabaqāti'l-Ḥanābilah*
- *Mukhtaṣar Sīrah 'Umar Ibn 'Abdu'l-'Azīz*

In exhortation his works include:

- *Laṭā'if al-Ma'ārif fīmā li-Mawāsim al-'Ām min al-Wadhā'if*
- *al-Farq baynan al-Naṣīḥah wat-Ta'yīr*
- *al-Takhwīf min al-Nār*
- *Aḥwāl Ahl ul-Qubūr*
- *Taḥqīq Kalimatu'l-Ikhlāṣ*

His Death

Ḥāfiẓ Ibn Rajab, may Allāh have mercy on him, died on a Monday night, the fourth of Ramaḍān 795H, while in Damascus.

His Published Works in English

Some of his fine works have been translated and published in English Language under the Dār as-Sunnah Ibn Rajab series:

- The Excellence of Knowledge
- Humility in Prayer
- The Journey to Allāh
- The Key to Paradise
- The Legacy of the Prophet
- The Heavenly Dispute
- The Journey of the Strangers
- Three that Follow the Deceased
- Difference between Advising and Shaming
- The Inheritors of the Prophets

THE AUTHOR'S INTRODUCTION

With the Name of Allāh, the All-Merciful, the Most Merciful

The Imām, may Allāh bestow His mercy upon him, said:

All praise is due to Allāh, Lord of all the worlds. His peace and blessings be upon Muḥammad, the seal of the Prophets, the leader of the pious,[1] the Messenger of the Lord of all the worlds, and upon his Family, his Companions and those that followed them until the Day of Judgment.

Imām Aḥmad[2], may Allāh have mercy upon him, transmitted from the ḥadīth of Mu'ādh Ibn Jabal (*raḍiyAllāhu 'anhu*), who said: 'The Messenger of Allāh (ﷺ) was held back from us once from the morning prayer, until we almost were face to face with the sun at its highest point. Then Messenger (ﷺ) came out to us quickly, he called for the prayer to be established and prayed shorter (than normal), when he finished, he said: "Stay in your rows."

[1] In another manuscript: *"Messengers."*

[2] Aḥmad in his *Musnad*, 5/243.

Then he turned to us and said: "I shall inform you the reason why I was delayed this morning. I stood for the night prayer and prayed as much as was written for me. Then I became drowsy in the prayer until sleep overtook me. Then all of a sudden, I woke up and lo and behold! I was with my Lord, the Mighty and Majestic, in the best of forms, He said to me: "O Muḥammad, what do you think the highest gatherings (of angels) are in dispute about?"

So I said: "I don't know my Lord."

He [again] said: "O Muḥammad, what do think the highest gatherings (of angels) are in dispute about?"

I replied: "I don't know my Lord."

He then said (for the third time): "O Muḥammad, what do you think the highest gatherings (of angels) are in dispute about?"

I [again] responded: "I don't know my Lord.

Then I saw Him place His palm between my shoulders until I felt the coldness of His fingertips reach my chest, then everything became clear to me and I came to know.

He asked [once again]: "O Muḥammad, what do you think the highest gatherings (of angels) are in dispute about?"

I said: "The actions that expiate (sins) and the (raising of the) ranks."

Then He asked: "What are the actions which expiate sins?"

I replied: "Taking steps towards the Friday prayers [to the *masājid* pl. masjid], sitting in the *masājid* after the prayers, and doing the ablution thoroughly even in[3] difficult conditions."

So then He said: "What are the ranks?"

I responded: "To feed others food, to have soft speech, and praying while the people are sleeping (the night prayer)."

Then He said to me: "Ask!, O Muḥammad."

So I said:

[3] In another manuscript: *"at"*

اللهم إني أسـألُك فعـلَ الخيرات، وتـركَ المنكرات، وحُبَّ
المسـاكين، وأنْ تغْفِـرَ لي وتَرْحَمَني، وإذا أردت فتنـةً في قومٍ
فتَـوفَّني غيرَ مفتـون، وأسألك حُبَّك وحُبَّ من يُحِبُّك وحُبَّ
عملٍ يقرِّبني إلى حبِّك»

"O Allāh I ask you (the ability to) do good actions, leaving bad actions, (having) love of the needy; that you forgive me and have mercy upon me. When you wish a calamity to befall a people to take my life without being put to trial. I ask you for your love and the love of the one who loves you and love of those actions that will draw me closer to your love."

Then Messenger of Allāh (ﷺ) said: "Indeed it is the truth, so study it and learn it."

Tirmidhī transmitted it[4] and said the ḥadīth is ḥasan ṣaḥīḥ.[6] He said: I asked Muḥammad Ibn Ismā'īl al-Bukhārī regarding this ḥadīth, he said: This ḥadīth is ḥasan ṣaḥīḥ.[6]

[4] Tirmidhī, #3235.

[5] In another manuscript: *"Authentic (ṣaḥīḥ)"*

[6] Tirmidhī transmitted in his *Sunan*, 5/344 the statement of Bukhārī: 'This is more authentic than the ḥadīth of Walīd Ibn Muslim from 'Abdu'l-Raḥmān Ibn Yazīd Ibn Jābir who said: Khālid Ibn Al-Lajlāj narrated to me that 'Abdu'l-Raḥmān Ibn 'Ā'ish Al-Khadramī said: I heard the Messenger of Allāh (ﷺ) then he mentioned the ḥadīth. This is not *maḥfūẓ*. Likewise Walīd mentioned in his narration from 'Abdu'l-Raḥmān Ibn 'Ā'ish who said: I heard the Messenger of Allāh (ﷺ). Bish Ibn Bakr narrated from 'Abdu'l-Raḥmān Ibn Yazīd Ibn Jābir this ḥadīth with this chain from 'Abdu'l-Raḥmān Ibn 'Ā'ish from the Prophet (ﷺ). And this is most authentic, and 'Abdu'l-Raḥmān Ibn 'Ā'ish did not hear from the Prophet (ﷺ). =

I say: In the chain of narration there is disagreement, and it has many routes, some have extra wording and others have less. I have mentioned most of the chains of narrations and some of the various wordings in the book: Explanation of Tirmidhī.

In some of its wording according to Imām Aḥmad[7] and Tirmidhī:[8] "Walking on foot to the congregation prayers" instead of "the Friday prayers."

Also they[9] have the wording after mentioning the expiating actions: "Whoever does so will live in good and die upon goodness. His sins will be as the day his mother gave birth to him."

In the wording[10] with them is also: "...and the ranks: To spread *salām* (Islāmic greeting)" instead of: "soft speech."

=

In the book *'Ilal Al-Kabīr* of Tirmidhī, #661. Tirmidhī said: I asked Muḥammad about this ḥadīth to which he replied: 'Abdu'l-Raḥmān Ibn 'Ā'ish did not meet the Prophet (ﷺ). And the narrations of Al-Walīd Ibn Muslim are not authentic.

The narration which is authentic is what was narrated by Jadham Ibn 'Abdullāh from Yaḥyā Ibn Abi Kathīr this narration of Mu'ādh Ibn Jabal (*raḍiyAllāhu 'anhu*).'

[7] Aḥmad in his *Musnad*, 5/378 from some of the Companions of the Prophet (ﷺ).

[8] Tirmidhī, #3233 on the authority of Ibn 'Abbās (*raḍiyAllāhu 'anhumā*).

Tirmidhī said: 'They mentioned between Abī Qilābah and Ibn 'Abbās (*raḍiyAllāhu 'anhu*) a man in this ḥadīth, and Qatadah narrated from Abi Qilābah from Khalid Ibn Al-Lajlāj from Ibn 'Abbās (*raḍiyAllāhu 'anhumā*).

[9] See previous two footnotes.

[10] Tirmidhī, #3233

In some narrations of the ḥadīth[11]: “I knew what was in the sky[12] and earth. Then he recited the verse:

وَكَذَٰلِكَ نُرِيٓ إِبۡرَٰهِيمَ
مَلَكُوتَ ٱلسَّمَٰوَٰتِ وَٱلۡأَرۡضِ وَلِيَكُونَ مِنَ ٱلۡمُوقِنِينَ ٧٥

“And thus did We showed Ibrāhīm the dominions of the heavens and the earth so that he might be one of the people of certainty [in faith].”

[*al-An'ām* (6): 75]

In another narration:

«. . . فتجلّى لي ما بين السماء والأرض.»

“So what was between the heaven and earth became clear to me.”[113]

And in another narration:

«ما بين المشرق والمغرب»

“...whatever is between the East and the West.”[114]

In some narrations there is an addition in the supplication which is contained in the ḥadīth:

---

[11] Ibn 'Āṣim in his *Al-Āhād wa'l-Mathanī*, #2585 with the wording: I knew what was in the heavens.

[12] In another manuscript: *Skies.*

[13] Al-Ruyānī in his *Musnad*, #656.

[14] Tirmidhī, #3234 on the authority of Ibn 'Abbās (*raḍiyAllāhu 'anhumā*), and Tirmidhī said: This ḥadīth is ḥasan garīb (good-strange) from this angle.

«. . . وتتـوب عـلَيَّ .»

"...and give me the ability to repent."[15]

And in another narration:

«إسباغ الوضوء في السَّـبرات»

"...to make ablution correctly passing water over the right places three times in the severe cold."[16]

In some other narration: 'And He said: 'O Muḥammad when you pray say:

اللهم إني أسـألُكَ فعـلَ الخيرات

"O Allāh I ask you the ability to do good deeds..."[17]

then the rest of the ḥadīth.

The purpose here [of this treatise] is to explain the ḥadīth and whatever can be extrapolated from it's knowledge (*mu'āriif*) and rulings (*aḥkām*) etc.

In this ḥadīth there is evidence that the Prophet (ﷺ) was not habitually late for the Morning Prayer (*ṣalāt al-fajr*) until nearer to

[15] Ibn 'Āṣim in his *al-Sunnah*, #388, and in *Al-Āhād wa'l-Mathani*, #2585.

[16] Bazzār in *al-Bahr al-Zukhār*, #2668, and Ṭabarānī in *Al-Kabīr*, 20/290, and *Al-Awsaṭ*, #5496.

[17] Tirmidhī, #3233. Refer to Darquṭnī's words on this ḥadīth in his book *'Illal*, 6/54-57 number, #973, Also the *'Illal Al-Mutanahiyah* of Ibn Al-Jawzī, 1/30-35. Darquṭnī mentioned the opposite of this regarding this ḥadīth and then said: There is nothing in it authentic, it is all self-contradictory. Ibn Al-Jawzī reported his speech and said: Abū Bakr Al-Bayhaqī said: Narrated from many angles of which all are weak.

sunrise, rather his habit (*'āda*) was to pray while it was still dark. He used to at times pray it while light had spread across the land, as for delaying it close to sunrise than that was not his normal practice, which is why he apologised in this ḥadīth.

It has been said: a delay to the extent that light has spread is not permissible unless for a reason (*'udhr*), and that it is a time of necessity (*ḍurūra*) such as delaying the 'Aṣr prayer until after the yellow light of the sun, and that is the statement of Al-Qāḍī from our companions in some of his books, and Imām Aḥmad has indicated as much, saying: 'This is the prayer of the one who has fallen short, this spread of light is when light has enveloped the earth.'

In this ḥadīth there is evidence that whoever delays the prayer until the very last part for a reason or something else, or fears the time period will finish while he is in the prayer if he prolongs it, than he can make it shorter so that he can make it within the time period.

As for the statement of Abū Bakr al-Ṣiddīq (*raḍiyAllāhu 'anhu*) when he made the Morning Prayer long and recited *Surah al-Baqarah* during it, it was said: the sun has almost risen. To which he replied: If it had risen it would not have found us unaware.[18]

Abū Bakr al-Ṣiddīq (*raḍiyAllāhu 'anhu*) did not intend to delay it until sunrise or to make it prolonged until then because when he started the prayer it was still dark. He lengthened the reading of the Qur'ān and was most likely engaged deeply in his recitation, so even if the sun had risen at that time it would not have harmed

[18] Bayhaqī in his *Sunan al-Kabīr*, 1/379, and in it was *Surah Āl-'Imrān* that was read.

him because it was not deliberate.

This shows that he held the view that the prayer was valid if the sun rose while a person is in prayer as the Prophet (ﷺ) ordered the one who had already prayed one rakʿah and the sun had risen to add another one.[19]

In the ḥadīth of Muʿādh (*raḍiyAllāhu ʿanhu*) there is proof that whoever has a dream that pleases him, then he should inform his companions and close friends that have love for him, especially if the dream involves good news for them, informing them of what benefits them. So the Prophet (ﷺ) after praying the Morning Prayer used to ask his Companions: "Who among you had a dream?"[20]

This ḥadīth also contains the fact that whoever becomes drowsy and sleeps during the night prayer, then sees a vision which is pleasing then that is a glad tiding.

From among the narrations of Al-Ḥasan that are *mursal*[21] is: When the servant [of Allāh] goes to sleep while he is in prostration, Allāh will vie with the angels out of pleasure with such servants saying: "O my angels look at my servant, his body is in my obedience and his soul is with me."

In this ḥadīth there is also a clear indication of the Prophet (ﷺ) honour (*sharf*) and merit (*tafḍīl*) by him knowing what is in the skies (or sky) and earth, and what the angels in the sky dispute

---

[19] Aḥmad in his *Musnad*, 2/489.

[20] Bukhārī, #1386 and Muslim, #2275 on the authority of Samarah (*raḍiyAllāhu ʿanhu*).

[21] Those that have a Companion missing in the chains

over became clear to him, as [Prophet] Ibrāhīm (*'alayhis-salām*) was shown the kingdom of the heavens and earth.

It has been reported in a narration directly from the Prophet[22] and in *mawqūf* form[23], that he was given knowledge of all things except the five keys of the unseen which are specific to Allāh's knowledge, as is mentioned in His statement:

إِنَّ ٱللَّهَ عِندَهُۥ عِلْمُ ٱلسَّاعَةِ وَيُنَزِّلُ ٱلْغَيْثَ
وَيَعْلَمُ مَا فِى ٱلْأَرْحَامِ ۖ وَمَا تَدْرِى نَفْسٌ مَّاذَا تَكْسِبُ غَدًا ۖ
وَمَا تَدْرِى نَفْسٌۢ بِأَىِّ أَرْضٍ تَمُوتُ ۚ إِنَّ ٱللَّهَ عَلِيمٌ خَبِيرٌۢ ﴿٣٤﴾

"Indeed, Allāh [alone] has knowledge of the Hour and it is He Who sends down the rain and He knows what is in the wombs. And no soul perceives what it will earn tomorrow."

[*Luqmān* (31): 34]

As for the description of the Prophet (ﷺ) of his Lord, the Most Majestic, then all of it is the truth and certain, which we must believe in and attest to. This is the same as what Allāh has described Himself, along with negating any similarities being made with Him. Whoever finds it difficult to understand any aspect of that or becomes confused should say as those people firmly grounded in knowledge [have said] and Allāh praised them for saying this when things become confusing for them:

[22] Aḥmad, 2/85-86 on the authority of Ibn 'Umar (*raḍiyAllāhu 'anhumā*) from the Prophet (ﷺ) directly. Haythamī said in *Al-Majma'*, 8/263 narrated by Aḥmad and Abū Ya'la and their men are the men of Bukhārī, and it is with Bukhārī, #1039 on the authority of Ibn 'Umar (*raḍiyAllāhu 'anhumā*).

Aḥmad, 1/386, 438, 445 and other on the authority of Ibn Mas'ūd.

[23] Not explicitly from the Prophet

ءَامَنَّا بِهِۦ كُلٌّ مِّنْ عِندِ رَبِّنَا

"We believe in it. All of it is from our Lord."

[*Āl-'Imrān* (3): 7]

As the Prophet (ﷺ) said in the Qur'ān: "And whatever you are unaware of then return it (the issue) back to the one that knows."

Reported by Imām Aḥmad[24] and Nasā'ī and among others, not over burdening oneself with something he has no knowledge of, for fear of destruction (*ḥalaka*) [for them selfs].

Ibn 'Abbās (*raḍiyAllāhu 'anhumā*) once heard someone narrating something from the Prophet (ﷺ) from these narrations then the man shook (his head) out of rejection of them, so Ibn 'Abbās (*raḍiyAllāhu 'anhumā*) said: 'What is the difference among these people? They find softness towards the things that are clear, but are destroyed due to those things that are ambiguous to them.' Reported by 'Abdu'l-Razzāq in his book[25] from Mu'im from Ibn Ṭāwūs, from his father on the authority of Ibn 'Abbās (*raḍiyAllāhu 'anhumā*).

Whenever the believers hear something from this type of speech they say: This is what Allāh has informed us with and His Messenger.

وَصَدَقَ ٱللَّهُ وَرَسُولُهُۥ ۚ وَمَا زَادَهُمْ إِلَّآ إِيمَٰنًا وَتَسْلِيمًا ﴿٢٢﴾

"Allāh and His Messenger have spoken the truth. It only increased them in faith and in submission."

[24] Aḥmad in his *Musnad*, 2/185 and in 2/181,300 with the wording *"return it to the one that knows"*

[25] As in *Al-Jami' Al-Mu'ammar*, 11/423 in *al-Mussanaf*, #20895.

The ḥadīth also shows that the *'high gathering'* (*al-mala' al-a'lā*) are angels (*malāika*) or those that have been drawn close (*muqarrabūn*) from them. Disputing among themselves, going back and forward with the statement about which actions (*a'māl*) draw the son of Adam closer to Allāh, the Mighty and Majestic, and expiates their sins. Allāh informs us that they also seek forgiveness (*istighfār*) for those that believe and supplicate for them.

In an authentic narration (it is mentioned): "Indeed when Allāh loves a servant he calls out: 'O Jibrīl, indeed I love such a person so you too love him. So Jibrīl loves that person and then he calls out in the sky: 'Indeed Allāh loves such a person so you too should love him.' So the inhabitants of the heavens love him too. Then acceptance for him is placed on earth.'"[26]

Abū Hurayrah (*raḍiyAllāhu 'anhu*) said: "When the son of Adam dies the people say: 'What has he left behind?' But the angels say: 'What did he put forward?'"[27]

So the angels ask about the actions of the sons of Adam because they hold it with much more importance and care.

So what remains now is what is intended by the ḥadīth which is: To mention the actions that expiate sins (*kafārāt*); the ranks (*darājāt*); supplications (*dawa'āt*). For each one we will divide them up into a separate chapter.

---

[26] Bukhārī, #3209 and Muslim, #2637.

[27] Bayhaqī in his *al-Shu'ab*, #10475 with the wording: "When a dead person dies, the angels say: 'What has he put forward, and the son of Adam says: 'What has he left behind.'"

CHAPTER ONE

Expiating Actions (*al-Kafārāt*)

It is to make ablution (*isbagh al-wuḍū*) in adverse and difficult conditions (*karīhāt*); walking (*aqdhām*) to the Friday prayers (*jumm'āt*) or any congregational prayers (*jāmā'āt*) and sitting (*julūs*) in the *masjids* after the prayer (*ṣalawāt*) is over.

They are called expiating actions (*kafārāt*) because they expiate sins (*khatāyā*) and bad deeds (*sayyi'āt*), so for this reason it is mentioned in some narrations: "Whoever does that will live with good, and die upon goodness. He will be like the day his mother gave birth to him."

These characteristics are mentioned mostly as expiating bad deeds (*takfīr al-sayyi'āt*), and also show how high ranks (*raf' al-darājāt*) are to be attained as is mentioned in Ṣaḥīḥ Muslim from the ḥadīth of Abū Hurayrah (*raḍiyAllāhu 'anhu*) from the Prophet (ﷺ) who said: "Shall I not inform you of those things that wipe away sins, and raise the ranks?"

They said: "Of course O Messenger of Allāh."

He replied: "To perform ablution over parts of the body in difficult conditions, regularly walking to the *masājid*, and waiting for the next prayer straight after the previous prayer [has finished]. Indeed, this is what should be held onto, this is what should be held onto."[28]

This meaning from the Prophet (ﷺ) is what has been narrated in many different forms. So there are three reasons (*thalāthat asbāb*) in expiating sins.

CHAPTER TWO

The First Reason for the Expiations of Sins: Making Ablution (*wuḍū*)

The Qur'ān has made clear the expiation of sins in the statement of Allāh, the Most High:

يَٰٓأَيُّهَا ٱلَّذِينَ ءَامَنُوٓاْ إِذَا قُمۡتُمۡ إِلَى ٱلصَّلَوٰةِ فَٱغۡسِلُواْ
وُجُوهَكُمۡ وَأَيۡدِيَكُمۡ إِلَى ٱلۡمَرَافِقِ وَٱمۡسَحُواْ بِرُءُوسِكُمۡ
وَأَرۡجُلَكُمۡ إِلَى ٱلۡكَعۡبَيۡنِۚ

"O you who believe! when you prepare for prayer wash your faces and hands up to your elbows, and wipe your heads and (wash) your feet up to the ankles."

Until

مَا يُرِيدُ ٱللَّهُ
لِيَجۡعَلَ عَلَيۡكُم مِّنۡ حَرَجٖ وَلَٰكِن يُرِيدُ لِيُطَهِّرَكُمۡ
وَلِيُتِمَّ نِعۡمَتَهُۥ عَلَيۡكُمۡ

"Allāh does not want to make things difficult for

you, but He wishes to purify you and complete His favour upon you."

[*al-Mā'idah* (5): 6]

So the statement: *'To purify you'* includes both purity of outer (*ṭahārah ẓāhir*) body with water, and the inner body (*ṭahārah bāṭin*) of sins (*dhunūb*), and the completion (*timām*) of His favour (*ni'ma*) is obtained by the forgiveness (*maghfira*) of sins and expiating them. Allāh said to His Prophet (ﷺ):

لِّيَغْفِرَ لَكَ ٱللَّهُ مَا تَقَدَّمَ مِن ذَنۢبِكَ
وَمَا تَأَخَّرَ وَيُتِمَّ نِعْمَتَهُۥ عَلَيْكَ وَيَهْدِيَكَ صِرَٰطًا مُّسْتَقِيمًا ﴿٢﴾

"So that Allāh may forgive you your earlier sins and any later ones and complete His favour upon you."

[*al-Fatḥ* (48): 2]

Muḥammad Ibn Ka'b al-Qurzī extrapolated this very meaning, and the ḥadīth reported by Tirmidhī[29] testifies to that affect, among others,[30] on the authority of Mu'ādh (*raḍiyAllāhu 'anhu*) that the Prophet (ﷺ) heard a man supplicate, saying:

اللهم إني أسألك تمام النعمة

'O Allāh I ask you of the completeness of your favour."

So he Prophet (ﷺ) said to him: "Do you know what the completeness of His favour is?" He said: 'It is a supplication from

[29] Tirmidhī, #3527 and said: This ḥadīth is ḥasan.

[30] Aḥmad, 5/231, 235, and Bukhārī in *Adab al-Mufrad*, #725, and Ṭabarānī in *Al-Kabīr*, 20/97, and Abū Nu'aym in *al-Ḥilyah*, 6/204. Abū Nu'aym said in *al-Ḥilyah*: He is alone in narrating from Lajlāj Abū'l-Ward, and then narrated too many of the major narrators from Al-Ḥarīrī from them: Isma'īl Ibn 'Illyah; Yazīd Ibn Zarī' and the two Imāms 'Alī Ibn Al-Madīnī and Aḥmad Ibn Ḥanbal.

which I hope good from.'

So the Prophet (ﷺ) said: "Indeed the completeness of the favour (*timām al-ni'ma*) is salvation from the fire (*najātu min al-nār*) and entering into Paradise (*dakhul al-jannah*)." So this favour cannot be complete for the servant (*'abd*) until his sins are expiated (*takfir al-sayyi'ah*).

There are many texts from the Prophet (ﷺ) regarding the expiation of sins by making ablution as is the case in Ṣaḥīḥ Muslim on the authority of 'Uthmān (*raḍiyAllāhu 'anhu*) who after making ablution said: "I saw the Messenger of Allāh (ﷺ) make ablution like this then he said: 'Whoever makes ablution like this will have his sins forgiven that he has sent forth, his prayer and walking to the masjid is also a form of extra worship.'"[31]

In another narration also from the Prophet (ﷺ) who said: "Whoever makes ablution and does it thoroughly, his sins will leave his body even from under his fingernails."[32]

Another narration from Abū Hurayrah (*raḍiyAllāhu 'anhu*) from the Prophet (ﷺ) who said: "When the Muslim servant, or believer, makes ablution and washes his face then all the sins he saw with his eyes leave his face along with the water, or with the last drop of water. When he washes his hands then all the sins he committed with his hands leave with the water, or with the last drop of water, until he becomes purified of all sins."[33]

---

[31] Muslim, #229.

[32] Muslim, #245.

[33] Muslim, #244.

From the narration of ʿAmr Ibn ʿAbassa (*raḍiyAllāhu ʿanhu*) also in Ṣaḥīḥ Muslim from the Prophet (ﷺ) who said: "There is no man amongst you that brings water for *wuḍū* near to himself for rinsing out his mouth and nose thoroughly with water except that his sins will leave him from his face and nose. Then when he washes his face as Allāh has ordered him until his sins leave him from every end of his beard as the water leaves. Then he washes his hands up to his elbows until his sins leave him from under his fingernails along with the water. Then he wipes his head until his sins leave him from all his hair along with the water. Then he washes his feet up to his ankles until his sins leave him from his toes. Then he stands up for prayer and praises Allāh, glorifies Him in a befitting way, he devotes his heart towards Allāh until he finishes, his sins would leave him as the day his mother gave birth to him."[34]

In the Muwaṭṭa;[35] the *Musnad* of Aḥmad;[36] the *Sunan* of Nasāʾī[37] and Ibn Mājah[38] from the narration of Sanābihī (*raḍiyAllāhu ʿanhu*) from the Prophet (ﷺ) who said: "When a believing servant makes *wuḍū* and puts water in his mouth his sins leave him from his mouth. When he puts water in his nose his sins leave him from his nose. When he washes his face his sins leave him from his face even from the lower parts of his eyes. When he washes his hands his sins leave him even from under his fingernails. When he wipes his head his sins leave him even from under his ears. When he washes

---

[34] Muslim, #832.

[35] Muwaṭṭa, 1/56, #30.

[36] Aḥmad in his *Musnad*, 4, #348, 349.

[37] Nasāʾī, 1, #74, 75.

[38] Ibn Mājah, #282.

his feet his sins leave him even from under his toenails, his walking to the *masjid* and his prayer are extra forms of worship."

In the *Musnad* from Abū Umāmah (*raḍiyAllāhu 'anhu*) from the Prophet (ﷺ) who said: "There is not a Muslim who makes *wuḍū*, washes his hands, gargles his mouth and makes *wuḍū* as Allāh has ordered him to, except that Allāh removes from him for that day: whatever his mouth has spoken, or his hands have touched, and what he has walked towards, until his sins leave him from his sides. When he walks to the *masjid,* for one step a good deed is written for him and for the other step a bad deed is removed."[39]

Furthermore the Prophet (ﷺ) said: "Any person who stands to make wuḍū intending to pray then washes his palms, his sins fall from his palms along with the first drop. When he washes his mouth and nose his sins fall from his tongue and lips along with the first drop. When he washes his face his sins fall from his hearing and sight along with the first drop. So when he washes his hands up to his elbows and feet up to his ankles he is free of every sin, along with every bad deed, [he becomes] as the day his mother gave birth to him. When he stands for prayer Allāh raises him a level and when he sits he sits in safety."[40]

This meaning is found in many other narrations, but what has

---

[39] I could not find it in the *Musnad,* it is with Ṭabarānī in *Al-Kabīr*, 8/7995 and he said: Al-Haythamī in *Al-Majma'*, 1/223. Narrated by Ṭabarānī in *Al-Kabīr* in the chain is: Laqīt Abū'l-Mūsāwir. Narrated by Abū Umāmah; and Al-Jarīrī Waqrah Ibn Khālid, and Ibn Ḥibbān mentioned it in *thiqāt,* and said he makes mistakes and contradicts.

[40] Aḥmad, 5/252,256,263,264. From all chains containing Shahr Ibn Hawshab and he is weak. Refer to *Al-Targhīb wa'l-Tarhīb* of Mundhirī, 1/155, and *Majma' al-Zawā'id* of Haythamī', 1/222-226.

been mentioned is sufficient. Many texts have also been reported concerning the reward of *wuḍū*, and this increases the expiation of sins further more. In Ṣaḥīḥ Muslim from 'Umar (*raḍiyAllāhu 'anhu*) from the Prophet (ﷺ) who said: "Whoever makes *wuḍū* and does so well, then he says:

(أشهدُ أن لا إله إلا الله ، وأن محمداً عبده ورسوله)

> 'I bear witness that there is no one worthy of worship except Allāh alone without any partner, and that Muḥammad is His slave and Messenger.'

All the eight doors of Paradise will open and he may enter from whichever one he pleases."[41]

Also in Ṣaḥīḥ Muslim from Abū Hurayrah(*raḍiyAllāhu 'anhu*) from the Prophet (ﷺ) who said: "The adornment of the believer (in Paradise) will reach the places where the water of *wuḍū* reaches (his body)."[42]

Also from the Prophet (ﷺ) who said: "You are like the white spot on the forehead of a horse because of making *wuḍū* properly."[43]

Reported by Bukhārī with the wording: "Indeed my nation will be called on the Day of Judgment with white spots on their foreheads like that of horses because of the effects of making *wuḍū*."[44]

---

[41] Muslim, #234.

[42] Muslim, #250.

[43] Muslim, #246.

[44] Bukhārī, #136.

Know that the ḥadīth of Mu'ādh Ibn Jabal (*raḍiyAllāhu 'anhu*) about the dream mentions [the virtues of] making *wuḍū* properly in difficult conditions.

Likewise in the ḥadīth of Abū Hurayrah (*raḍiyAllāhu 'anhu*) which has been mentioned at the start of this chapter. There are two issues here: One of them: Making *wuḍū* properly (*isbāgh*), which means to complete the *wuḍū* and the water must reach every places that are legally set [in the religion]. As reported in the *Musnad* of Al-Bazzār[45] from 'Uthmān (*raḍiyAllāhu 'anhu*) [in *marfu* form] directly from the Prophet (ﷺ) who said: "Whoever does *wuḍū* and does it properly his past and future sins are forgiven."

The chain of narration is acceptable, and it is reported by Ibn Abī 'Āṣim[46] from another chain also from 'Uthmān (*raḍiyAllāhu 'anhu*).

Reported by Nasā'ī[47] and Ibn Mājah[48] from the ḥadīth of Abū Mālik Al-'Ashari (*raḍiyAllāhu 'anhu*) from Prophet (ﷺ) who said: "Making *wuḍū* properly is half of faith (*shatrul-īmān*)."

[Reported by Muslim[49] with the wording: "Purification is half of faith (*shatrul-īmān*)."]

---

[45] Bazzār, #262—*Kashf* and similar.
Haythamī said in *Al-Majma'*, 1/237: The men in the chain of narrations are all reliable and the ḥadīth is good if Allāh wills. Likewise Al-Mundhirī in *Al-Targhīb wa'l-Tarhīb*, 1/103.

[46] I was not able to find it. However, a similar longer version is found on the authority of Abi Al-Darda' in Ibn Abi Aasim, ('Al-Aahad al-Mathani'), #2040.

[47] *Al-Mujtabah* 5/5.

[48] Ibn Mājah, #280.

[49] Muslim, #223.

The second: That the completeness (of *wuḍū*) in difficult conditions. The meaning of this refers to a situation where the person dislikes making *wuḍū*, due to befalling of calamities (*nuzūl al-maṣā'ib*) which makes a person despair, so being preoccupied away from that with patience (*ṣabr*), to perform the *wuḍū* and the prayer (*ṣalah*) is a sign of faith (*'alāmatul-īmān*), as Allāh says:

وَٱسْتَعِينُوا۟ بِٱلصَّبْرِ وَٱلصَّلَوٰةِ ۚ وَإِنَّهَا لَكَبِيرَةٌ إِلَّا عَلَى ٱلْخَٰشِعِينَ

"Seek help in patience and in the prayer, it is difficult except for those that are devout."

[*al-Baqarah* (2): 45]

And the statement of the Most High:

يَٰٓأَيُّهَا ٱلَّذِينَ
ءَامَنُوا۟ ٱسْتَعِينُوا۟ بِٱلصَّبْرِ وَٱلصَّلَوٰةِ ۚ إِنَّ ٱللَّهَ مَعَ ٱلصَّٰبِرِينَ ﴿١٥٣﴾

"O you who believe! seek help in patience and prayer. Indeed, Allāh is with those that have patience."

[*al-Baqarah* (2): 153]

The *wuḍū* is the key to the prayer (*miftāḥ al-ṣalah*), and the heat of the heart (*ḥararat al-qalb*) that emanates from the pain of calamities (*alam al-masā'ib*) is extinguished, like the one who becomes enraged (*ghadab*) is ordered to extinguish (*itfā'*) his rage by making *wuḍū*.

The disliked places (*karīhāt*) is also explained as severe cold (*bard al-shadīd*), which is something that the ḥadīth of Mu'ādh (*raḍiyAllāhu 'anhu*) testifies to "Making *wuḍū* in severely cold conditions [*sabrah*—being severe cold]". No doubt that making *wuḍū* in the cold is difficult for the soul and painful. Anything that causes pain to the soul and is difficult, is an expiation of sins. In some cases the person may not be the cause of it, such as illness that may effect a person, which many texts indicate.

As for the pain that comes about because of an action that is in obedience (*ṭā'ṭ*) to Allāh, then the person will be rewarded, and his rank (*darajah*) will be raised. As is the pain felt by the one striving (*mujāhada*) in the way of Allāh, the Most High. As Allāh, the Most High says:

ذَٰلِكَ بِأَنَّهُمْ لَا يُصِيبُهُمْ ظَمَأٌ وَلَا نَصَبٌ
وَلَا مَخْمَصَةٌ فِي سَبِيلِ ٱللَّهِ وَلَا يَطَـُٔونَ مَوْطِئًا يَغِيظُ
ٱلْكُفَّارَ وَلَا يَنَالُونَ مِنْ عَدُوٍّ نَّيْلًا إِلَّا كُتِبَ لَهُم
بِهِۦ عَمَلٌ صَٰلِحٌ ۚ إِنَّ ٱللَّهَ لَا يُضِيعُ أَجْرَ ٱلْمُحْسِنِينَ ﴿١٢٠﴾

"That is because no thirst or fatigue or hunger will afflict them in the cause of Allāh, nor do they take a single step to infuriate the unbelivers, nor do they secure any gain from the enemy or take something from them, except it is written for them as a good deed. Surely, Allāh does not wast the reward of the doers of good."

[*al-Tawbah* (9): 120]

Likewise pain (*alam*); hunger (*ju'*) and thirst (*'atsh*) which the fasting person (*ṣā'im*) gets, is the same as making ablution (*isbagh al-wuḍū*) in the cold. Patience (*ṣabr*) must be resorted in order to overcome such pain, and if pleasure (*riḍā*) is obtained then that is a special station (*maqām khawāṣ*) of those that know and have love (*al-'ārifīn al-muḥibīn*). This pleasure only comes to fruition if the following issues are observed:

The first of them: is to remember the virtue of ablution (*faḍl al-wuḍū*) and how it removes sins, raises the ranks (*darajāt*); and gaining the whiteness (purity) from it; and the adornment in paradise covering a person where the water of *wuḍū* reached. In this way one of the pious women of the past humbled herself in order to find (this pleasure). After braking her finger nail she smiled and said: 'The sweetness of the reward (*ḥalāwa al-thawab*) made me forget the bitterness of the pain (*murāra waja'*).'

One of the people who had knowledge said: 'Whoever does not know the reward of the actions (*thawab al-a'māl*), then all actions will become difficult for him, in all circumstances (*jamī' al-aḥwāl*).'

Secondly: A knowledgeable person once said: 'Remember what Allāh has prepared for the one that disobeys Him from the severe cold punishment (*al-'adhab bi'l-bard wa'l-zamharīr*), for indeed the severity of the cold in this world reminds us of the cold of the Hell-fire (*jahanam*)'. In an authentic ḥadīth it mentions: "Indeed the most severe cold that you will find is the coldness of the Hell-fire."[50]

So observing this cold that is promised makes less significant any other feeling of pain from cold water, as has been narrated from Zabīd Al-Yāmī that he once stood at night to pray while it was very cold. When he put his hand in a container and found it was very cold he remembered the severe cold of the Hell-fire, and he never felt the cold of this world again after that. His hand remained in the water until morning, so his slave girl said to him: 'What's wrong, you did not pray at night as you usually do?'

He said: 'I found the water to be very cold, but I remembered

[50] Bukhārī, #536 and Muslim, #617.

the coldness of the Hell-fire and I never felt the coldness [again], so my hand remained until the morning, do not inform anyone as long as I am alive.'

Thirdly: One should observe the greatness (*jalāl*) of the one who has ordered the *wuḍū*, His majesty (*'aẓma*) and grandeur (*kibriyā'*). Remember preparing to stand in front of Him and conversing with Him in the prayer (*ṣalah*), because it lessens the pain the servant suffers of cold water in order to gain the pleasure of Allāh. May be one does not even feel the coldness of the water as some of the people that have awareness said: 'With knowledge worship becomes easier.'

Sa'īd Ibn 'Amir said: 'It has reached me that [Prophet] Ibrāhīm (*'alayhis-salām*) used to make wuḍū while his bones were trembling.'

When 'Alī Ibn Al-Ḥusayn (*raḍiyAllāhu 'anhu*) used to make *wuḍū* his colour would change to yellow, so it was said to him: 'What happens to you when you make *wuḍū*?' He would say: 'Do you know in front of whom I intend to stand?'

Manṣūr Ibn Zādān would cry after finishing from making *wuḍū* until his voice became loud, so it was said to him (in another manuscript: It would be said to him): 'What is the matter with you?' So he said: '(in another manuscript: He would say) what is greater than my matter. I want to stand in front of the one who does not get tired or sleep, perhaps He will turn away from me.'[51]

When 'Aṭā' al-Sulaimī finished from making *wuḍū* he would shake, tremble and weep profusely, so it was mentioned to him about that, to which he replied: 'Indeed I want to go forth for an important

[51] In the printed edition: He would be pleased with me.

matter, I want to stand before Allāh, the Mighty and Majestic.'

Fourthly: To be conscious that Allāh is aware of the servant's state when he is doing actions for Him, and the difficulty he endures for His sake. So whoever has certainty (*yaqīn*) that afflictions are under the watchful eye of the One who loves him, all the pain becomes easy upon him, as is indicated by the Most High, in his statement to His Prophet (ﷺ):

وَٱصۡبِرۡ لِحُكۡمِ رَبِّكَ فَإِنَّكَ بِأَعۡيُنِنَاۖ

"So be patient with the command of your Lord, for indeed your well within Our sight."

[*al-Ṭūr* (52): 48]

And the statement of the Most High to [Prophet] Mūsā and [Prophet] Harūn (*'alayhis-salām*):

قَالَ لَا تَخَافَآۖ إِنَّنِي مَعَكُمَآ أَسۡمَعُ وَأَرَىٰ

"Have no fear. Verily! I am with both of you; I hear and I see (everything)."

[*Ṭāhā* (20): 46]

The Prophet (ﷺ) said: "Worship Allāh as if you see Him, and though you do not see Him, He indeed sees you."[52]

Abū Sulaymān al-Daranī said: 'I have read in some books that: Allāh, the Mighty and Majestic says: 'In My sight are the ones that tolerate things for My sake. Those who endure suffering to seek My pleasure. How would they be when they come to Me and live in comfort in My eternal gardens?'

---

[52] Bukhārī, #50, and Muslim, #8 in the context of the long ḥadīth of Jibrīl (*'alayhis-salām*).

There are glad tidings for those who purify their actions for Allāh, of an amazing spectacle from the close and loving One. Do you think that I will waste any of their actions?

So how (is it that if) I am generous with those that turn away from me, then how would I be with those that come towards me?

So making *wuḍū* properly in the cold, especially at night, will be done with Allāh's full knowledge, He will be pleased with it, show His pleasure to the angels that are with Him, so be conscious of that and that will lessen the pain.

In the *Musnad*,[53] and Ṣaḥīḥ Ibn Ḥibbān[54] it is reported from 'Uqbah Ibn 'Amir (*raḍiyAllāhu 'anhu*) from the Prophet (ﷺ) who said: "There are two types of men in my *ummah*, one of them stands up in the night to purify himself and he has knots over him. So when he makes *wuḍū*, he washes his hands one of the knots is untied, when he washes his face another knot is untied, when he wipes his head another knot is untied, and when he washes his feet another knot is untied. So the Lord, the Mighty and the Majestic, says to those behind the veil: 'Look at my servant trying to purify himself. Whatever this servant of mine asks me, will be his...' Then he mentioned the rest of the ḥadīth.

Narrated by 'Atiyyah from Abū Sa'īd from the Prophet (ﷺ)who said: "Indeed Allāh laughs at three types of people: A man that

[53] Aḥmad in his *Musnad*, 4/159,201, and Haythamī said in *Al-Majma'*, 1/224 from the second: Its chain of narrators are reliable

[54] Ibn Ḥibbān, #168—*Mawārid*.

stands up in the middle of the night, does *wuḍū* well and prays..."[55] and he mentioned the rest of the ḥadīth.

One of the Salaf used to have a set amount that he would read during the night, but he became weary once when he heard a voice saying:

'Under the watchful gaze of Allāh during the night, the servants made their standing, driven to serve Him.'

Fifthly: Immersing oneself (*istighrār*) in loving (*maḥabba*) the One who orders His obedience (*ṭā't*), for that He is pleased with it and loves it, as Allāh, the Most High says:

إِنَّ ٱللَّهَ يُحِبُّ ٱلتَّوَّٰبِينَ وَيُحِبُّ ٱلْمُتَطَهِّرِينَ ﴿٢٢٢﴾

"Indeed, Allāh loves those who turn unto Him constantly and He loves those that purify themselves."
[*al-Baqarah (2): 222*]

So whoever fills his heart (*qalb*) with the love of Allāh, the Mighty and Majestic, loves what He loves, even if it is difficult, and one feels the pain as a result, it has been said: 'Love makes easy heavy burdens.'

One of the Salaf said during his illness: 'What is most beloved to me is what is most beloved to Him.'

Similarly it has been said:

[55] Al-Bazzār, #715—*Kashf* from Muḥammad Ibn 'Abdu'l-Raḥmān Ibn Abī Layla from 'Atiyyah Al-'Awfi, and Haythamī said in *Al-Majma'*, 2/256 in it is Muḥammad Ibn Abī Layla and there is much speech about his bad memory but not because of lying.

What is injury if pain brings pleasure?

And:

Your love will lessen what arises,
The one who has not been distressed, does not enjoy bliss.

So whoever serves the one he loves, then he finds pleasure even when he is disappointed during his servitude of the one he loves.

One of them said: 'The heart that loves for Allāh's sake, loves to exert himself for Him.'

'Abdu'l-Samad said: 'He places for them in His punishment sweetness for the difficulties they endure for His sake.'

So making *wuḍū* properly in difficult conditions is a sign of those that love as it has mentioned in *"Kitāb al-Zuhd"* of Imām Aḥmad[56] from 'Aṭā' Ibn Yasār said: 'Mūsā (*'alayhis-salām*) said: 'O Lord who are your very special servants?'

He said: 'They are those whose hands are free of blame (bodies, in another manuscript), and their hearts are pure. Those that love each other for My Majesty. Those that when I am mentioned they remember Me, and when they are mentioned I remember them. Those that do *wuḍū* properly in difficult conditions, and frequently remember me, as frogs frequently enter their nests. They are fond of my love, as a child is fond of love from people. They are enraged when what I have forbidden, is made permissible, like a tiger in battle.'

For those that have this love, Allāh may aid them through a

[56] Aḥmad in his *Musnad*, p.74-75, between 'Aṭā' and Mūsā (*'alayhis-salām*) are inhospitable deserts that can break the necks of riding beasts.

miracle, some of them might not feel the coldness of cold water. Others would to supplicate to Allāh to make easy the purification in winter, so when the water was brought to them it would be warm. Yet some would not feel anything at all of the warmth or the coldness.

'Alī Ibn Abī Ṭālib (*raḍiyAllāhu 'anhu*) had the Prophet (ﷺ) supplicate for him to take away the ability to feel cold and heat, so he used to wear in the summer winter clothes, and in the winter he would ware summer clothes.[57]

The Prophet (ﷺ) said about him: "Indeed he loves Allāh and His Messenger, and he is loved by Allāh and His Messenger."[58]

Abū Sulaymān al-Daranī on his way to *ḥajj* saw an old man wearing shabby clothes in severe cold, all the while he was sweating. So he asked him about his state. He replied: 'The heat and cold are two creations of Allāh, the Mighty and Majestic, so if he orders them to overwhelm me then it will befall me, and if He orders them to leave me then they will.' He also said: 'I have been in this wilderness for thirty years. He covers me in winter out of His love, and in the summer cools me out of His love.' It was said to someone else who had two rags to cover himself in the severe cold: 'If you covered yourself it would save you from the cold,' so he replied:

'I hope for only good in His courtyard,
for does anyone feel cold in His shelter?'

[57] Ibn Mājah, #117, Al-Buṣayrī said in *Zawā'id*, 1/70: This has a weak chain of narration, Ibn Abi Layla Shaikh Wakī' who is Muḥammad is weak in memory and not used when he is alone in a narration, also reported by Ṭabarānī in *Al-Awsaṭ*, #2286 and Haythamī said in *Al-Majma'*, 9/122: The chain is ḥasan.

[58] Bukhārī, #3009 and Muslim, #2406.

CHAPTER THREE

The Second Reason for the Expiations of Sins: Walking to the Congregation and Friday prayers

More specifically, if a person makes *wuḍū* at home and then leaves to go to the masjid, intending nothing other than the prayer as it has reported in the both Bukhārī and Muslim on the authority of Abū Hurayrah (*raḍiyAllāhu 'anhu*) from the Prophet (ﷺ) who said: "The reward of a person praying in congregation compared to at home or in the market place, is twenty five times greater. That is because when he makes *wuḍū* properly and leaves his house for no other reason but the prayer in the *masjid*. Every step he takes he is raised a rank, and a bad deed is wiped away from him. So when he prays, the angels continue to send peace and blessings upon him as long as he is in place of prayer saying: 'O Allāh send peace and blessings upon him, O Allāh have mercy upon him, and as long as you are waiting for a prayer you will be considered in prayer.'"[59]

It is reported in the Ṣaḥīḥ Muslim on the authority of Abū Hurayrah (*raḍiyAllāhu 'anhu*) from the Prophet (ﷺ) who said:

[59] Bukhārī, #647 and Muslim, #649.

"Whoever purifies himself at home, then walks to the houses of Allāh to perform an obligation from the (many) obligations Allāh (has placed upon him). Then every two steps (or 'steps' in another manuscript) he takes, one step removes a bad deed and another step raises his level."[60]

In the Two Ṣaḥīḥs on the authority of Abū Hurayrah (*raḍiyAllāhu 'anhu*) from the Prophet (ﷺ) who said: "Every step taken to the prayer is a charity."[61]

In the *Musnad*[62] and Ṣaḥīḥ Ibn Ḥibbān[63] on the authority of 'Uqbah Ibn 'Amir (*raḍiyAllāhu 'anhu*) who reported from the Prophet (ﷺ) who said: "When a person purifies himself, then goes to the *masjid* to take care of his prayer, his two scribes write for him with every step he takes to the *masjid* as ten good deeds.[64]

It is also reported in Ibn Ḥibbān and the *Musnad* on the authority of 'Abdullāh Ibn 'Amr (*raḍiyAllāhu 'anhu*) from the Prophet (ﷺ) who said: "Whoever goes to the *masjid* for congregation, then for

[60] Muslim, #666.

[61] This is not in the Two Ṣaḥīḥs of Bukhārī and Muslim with this wording from Abū Hurayrah (*raḍiyAllāhu 'anhu*), rather it is reported by Aḥmad, 2/312,316,350.

[62] Aḥmad in his *Musnad*, 4/157.

[63] Ibn Ḥibbān, #2045—*Iḥsān*

[64] Al-Mundhirī said in *Al-Targhīb*, 1/207 about this ḥadīth: Some of its chains are authentic. Haythamī said in *Al-Majma'*, 2/29: Narrated by Aḥmad and Abū Ya'la and Ṭabarānī in *Al-Kabīr* and *Al-Awsaṭ*, and in some chains of narration is Ibn Lahi'ah, some of them are authentic made so by Al-Ḥākim. I said: The wording is Ḥākim's in *Al-Mustadrak*, 1/211. This ḥadīth is authentic according to Muslim's criterion but they never reported it.

every two steps he takes, one step wipes away sin, and the other is written as a good deed, going and returning (from the masjid)."[65]

In the *Sunan* of Abū Dāwūd on the authority of Abū Umāmah (*raḍiyAllāhu 'anhu*) from the Prophet (ﷺ) who said: "Whoever leaves his house purified for the obligatory prayer then his reward is like that of a pilgrim."[66]

Furthermore, it is also reported from a man among the Al-Anṣar from the Prophet (ﷺ) who said: "Whoever makes *wuḍū* properly, then leaves for the prayer, does not raise his right foot except Allāh writes for him a single good deed, and he does not put down his left foot except Allāh removes a bad deed from him, so you may reside close or far, as long as he comes to the masjid and prays in congregation he will be forgiven."[67]

The narrations in this regard are many.

Walking to the Friday prayer has even more virtue, especially after *wuḍū* is made, as reported in the *Sunan* on the authority of Aws Ibn Aws (*raḍiyAllāhu 'anhu*) from the Prophet (ﷺ) who said: "Whoever takes a bath on Friday, and bathes completely. Leaves early, arriving early. Walks and does not ride (to the *masjid*). Sits close to the Imām and listens to him, and does not engage in idle talk - for every step he takes he will have the reward of one year,

[65] Aḥmad in his *Musnad*, 2/172, and Ibn Ḥibbān, #419—*Mawārid*. Haythamī said in *Al-Majma*', 2/29. Narrated by Aḥmad and Ṭabarānī in *Al-Kabīr*, and the narrators are of Ṭabarānī and are narrators of Bukhārī and Aḥmad, among them Ibn Lahi'ah.

[66] Abū Dāwūd, #558.

[67] Abū Dāwūd, #563.

the reward of a year's fasting and praying (at night)."[68]

The further away he lives from the *masjid* then his walking is better because of the more steps he has to take.

In the Ṣaḥīḥ of Muslim on the authority of Jābir (*raḍiyAllāhu 'anhu*) reported: 'Our house was far from the masjid and we wanted to sell our houses to move closer to the masjid, so the Prophet (ﷺ) forbade us saying: "for every step you take is a good deed." [69] In the Ṣaḥīḥ of Bukhārī from Anas that the Prophet (ﷺ) said: "O sons of Salāmah! Will you not count your steps?"'[70]

In Ṣaḥīḥ Bukhārī and Muslim on the authority of Abū Mūsā (*raḍiyAllāhu 'anhu*) who reported that the Prophet (ﷺ) said: "Indeed the people with the most reward for the prayer are those that walk the furthest to get to it."[71]

Having said this, the house that is close to the masjid is better than the house that is distant, however walking from the house that is further distance away is better.

In the *Musnad* on the authority of Hudayfah (*raḍiyAllāhu 'anhu*) reported from the Prophet (ﷺ) who said: "The virtue of a house that is close to the masjid over the house that is distant and faraway is like the virtue of the warrior over the one sitting down."

---

[68] Abū Dāwūd, #345, #346, Tirmidhī, #496 and he said it is ḥasan. Nasa'ī, 3/95, 96, 97, and Ibn Mājah, #1087.

[69] Muslim, #664.

[70] Bukhārī, #655.

[71] Bukhārī, #651 and Muslim, #662.

The chain is broken.[72]

Walking to the *masjid* is better than riding as has preceded from the ḥadīth of Aws (*raḍiyAllāhu 'anhu*) for the Friday prayer. For this reason the ḥadīth of Mu'ādh (*raḍiyAllāhu 'anhu*) mentions the superiority of walking. The Prophet (ﷺ) used to not leave for the prayer, except by walking, even the *'Īd* prayer he would go to walking. Hence the one who comes to the *masjid* is a visitor to Allāh, and visiting someone on foot is closer to humbleness (*khudu'*) and lowering oneself (*tadhlil*), as it has been said:

If I came to you as a visitor in a rush,
I would not even then fulfil the right.

It is reported in Ṣaḥīḥ Bukhārī on the authority of Abū Hurayrah (*raḍiyAllāhu 'anhu*) from the Prophet (ﷺ) who said: "Whoever goes out to the *masjid* in the morning or evening, Allāh prepares for him in paradise a *nuzul,* every time he goes out in the morning or evening."[73]

"Nuzl" is a banquet prepared for a guest when one arrives.

It has been recorded in Ṭabarānī[74] from the ḥadīth of Salmān

---

[72] Aḥmad in his *Musnad,* 5/387 Haythamī said in *Al-Majma',* 2/16: Aḥmad narrated it and in the chain is Ibn Lahi'ah and there is speech about him. I said: In the chain is Abū 'Abdu'l-Mālik and he is 'Alī Ibn Yazīd, Al-Albānī said along with his weakness, his narrations from Hudayfah (*raḍiyAllāhu 'anhu*) have broken chains of narration.

[73] Bukhārī, #66.

[74] Ṭabarānī in *Al-Kabir,* 6/311-312 and Al-Mundhirī, 1/214, said: Narrated by Ṭabarānī with two chains of narrations one of which is good and Haythamī, 2/31: One of the chains has narrators of Bukhārī.

(*raḍiyAllāhu ʿanhu*) directly from the Prophet (ﷺ) who said: "Whoever makes *wuḍū* in his house and does so properly. Then he goes to the *masjid,* he is a visitor of Allāh, the Most High, and the right of the visitor on the one being visited is that he honours him."

It is reported in Ṣaḥīḥ Muslim on the authority of Ubay Ibn Kaʿb (*raḍiyAllāhu ʿanhu*) who said: "There was a man who lived the furthest away from the *masjid,* and he never missed a prayer in the *masjid.* So it was said to him (or I said to him): 'Why don't you get a donkey and ride it to the *masjid* in the darkness and intense heat.' So he replied: 'It would not please me to have my house next to the *masjid.* I would prefer that my walking to the *masjid* and return to my family be written down in my favour.' So the Prophet (ﷺ) said: "Allāh will gather all of that for you."[75]

Further more the walking that is difficult to the *masjid,* is far better and one is greatly rewarded for it. Hence the virtue of walking to the *masjid* for the night prayer and the morning prayer, is equal to standing in prayer all night as reported in Ṣaḥīḥ Muslim on the authority of ʿUthmān (*raḍiyAllāhu ʿanhu*) from the Prophet (ﷺ) who said: "Whoever prays *ʿIshā* in congregation is as if he stood praying half the night, and whoever prays the morning prayer in congregation then it is as if he has prayed the whole night standing."[76]

In Bukhārī and Muslim, it is reported on the authority of Abū Hurayrah (*raḍiyAllāhu ʿanhu*) from the Prophet (ﷺ) who said: "The most difficult prayers for the hypocrites are the *ʿIshā* and *Fajr* prayers. If they knew the reward for attending them, they would come even if they had to crawl."

[75] Muslim, #663.

[76] Muslim, #644.

The reason why these two prayers are difficult for the hypocrites (*munafiqūn*) is because the hypocrite is only active for the prayer, when people are watching him. Allāh, the Most High says:

إِنَّ ٱلْمُنَٰفِقِينَ يُخَٰدِعُونَ ٱللَّهَ وَهُوَ خَٰدِعُهُمْ وَإِذَا قَامُوٓا۟ إِلَى
ٱلصَّلَوٰةِ قَامُوا۟ كُسَالَىٰ يُرَآءُونَ ٱلنَّاسَ وَلَا يَذْكُرُونَ ٱللَّهَ إِلَّا
قَلِيلًا ﴿١٤٢﴾

> **"Behold, the hypocrites think they deceive Allāh, but He is deceiving them. When they stand up for the prayer, they stand up lazily, to be seen and showing off to people, only remembering Allāh a very little."**
>
> [*al-Nisā'* (4): 142]

Both the *'Ishā* and the Morning Prayer (*fajr*) occur in the dark. So only the truly sincere person (*mukhliṣ*) will be active enough to walk towards them, suffice in the knowledge that Allāh, the Mighty and Majestic will alone see him.

The reward for walking to the *masjid* in the darkness (*ẓulm*) is: Complete light (*nūr tām*) during the darkness of the Day of Judgment (*ẓulm al-qiyāmah*) as reported in the *Sunan* of Abū Dāwūd[78] and Tirmidhī[79] on the authority of Buraydah (*raḍiyAllāhu 'anhu*) from the Prophet (ﷺ) who said: "Give glad tidings to the people that walk in darkness to the masjids, they will have complete light on the Day of Judgment."

[77] Bukhārī, #644 and Muslim, #651.

[78] Abū Dāwūd, #561.

[79] Tirmidhī, #223 and he said: This ḥadīth is strange from this chain.

It has been reported by Ibn Mājah[80] from the ḥadīth of Sahl Ibn Sa'd (*raḍiyAllāhu 'anhu*), and it has been narrated from many chains of narrations.[81]

[80] Ibn Mājah, #780

[81] From the narrations of:

1. Anas (raḍiyAllāhu 'anhu): Reported by Ibn Mājah, #422 and Ibn Al-Jawzī said in *'Ilal Al-Mutanahiyah*, 1/406: In the chain are unknown people and Al-Būṣāyrī said in *Al-Zawā'id*, 1/100 the ḥadīth is weak.
2. Abū Dardā' (*raḍiyAllāhu 'anhu*): In Ibn Ḥibbān, #422—*Mawārid.* Al-Haythamī said in *Al-Majma'*, 2/30, it has Janād Ibn Abī Khālid whose biography I was not able to find, the other narrators are reliable.
3. Abū Sa'īd Al-Khudrī (*raḍiyAllāhu 'anhu*): It is reported by Al-Ṭayalisī, #2212, and Al-'Uqailī, 3/105 and Ibn 'Adī, 5/334. Al-'Uqailī said about this narration: it has in it *Līn.* Ibn 'Adī said: 'Abdu'l-Ḥakam has other narrations not mentioned, and his ḥadīth are generally not to be followed, and some of the texts are narrated by the famous (narrators) except with the chain mentioned by 'Abdu'l-Ḥakam maybe he did not narrate that. Ibn Al-Jawzī said *'Ilal Al-Mutanahiyah*, 1/408: This is not authentic, and Ibn Ḥibbān said: It is not allowed to write down the ḥadīth of 'Abdu'l-Ḥakam except to wonder at them.
4. Abū Hurayrah (*raḍiyAllāhu 'anhu*): It is reported by Ibn Mājah, #779. Al-Būṣāyrī said: This ḥadīth is weak, Abū Rafī' agreed to its weakness; Al-Walīd Ibn Muslim is a Mudalis and used the word "*'an'*.
5. 'Ā'ishah (*raḍiyAllāhu 'anhā*): It is reported by Ṭabarānī in *Al-Awsaṭ*, #1275 and said: No one narrated this ḥadīth from 'Atā' from 'Ā'ishah (*raḍiyAllāhu 'anhā*) except Al-Ḥasan, and Qatadah was alone in doing so. Haythamī said in *Al-Majma'*, 1/30: In the chain is Al-Ḥasan Ibn 'Alī Al-Sharuwī. Al-Dhahabī said: He is not known and in his narration is someone unknown, Al-'Uqaili said: He is not to be followed.
6. Abū Umāmah (*raḍiyAllāhu 'anhu*): It is reported by Ṭabarānī in *Al-Kabīr*, 8/7633, 7634, 8125.
7. 'Umar (*raḍiyAllāhu 'anhu*): Reported by Ibn Al-Jawzī in *'Ilal Al-Mutanahiyah*, #683 who said: This ḥadīth has not been established.
8. Ibn 'Umar (*raḍiyAllāhu 'anhumā*): It is reported by Ṭabarānī in *Al-Kabīr*, 12/13335.
9. Zayd Ibn Ḥarithah (*raḍiyAllāhu 'anhu*): It is reported by Ṭabarānī in *Al-Kabīr*, 5/4662. Haythamī said in *Al-Majma'*, 2/30: It is narrated by Ṭabarānī

In some narrations there is the addition: 'The (other) people will be frightened, but they will not be.'[82]

Al-Nakha'ī said: 'They used to hold the view that walking in the dark at night would necessitate a person being forgiven.'

It is narrated from Al-Ḥasan who said: 'The people of *tawḥīd* (*ahlul-tawḥīd*) in the hell fire will not be tied up, so the guardians (angels) will say to each other why is it that these people are not tied up, while others are tied up?' So a caller will call out to them: 'These people are those that use to walk to the *masjids* during the dark nights.'

Just as the places of prostration (*mawādi' al-sujūd*) of the sinful Muslim, among the people of *tawḥīd* (*al-muwaḥidūn*) in the hell fire, are not devoured by the fire of hell. Likewise the feet that walk to the masjids in the dark will not be tied in the fire. Nor will the punishment be equal for the one who served Him and the one who did not serve Him.

'So (if this is the case) the one who has earned His anger,
He still treats them with goodness.
What would be the case for the one who only pleased Him?'

=

in *Al-Awsaṭ* and in *Al-Kabīr*, and in the chain is Ibn Lahi'ah and people are in disagreement about using him.

10. Ibn 'Abbās (*raḍiyAllāhu 'anhumā*): reported by Ṭabarānī in *Al-Kabīr*, 10/10689, Haythamī said in *Al-Majma'*, 2/30: It is reported by Ṭabarānī in *Al-Kabīr* and in the chain is Al-'Abbās Ibn 'Amir. Dhahabī said: I could not find his biography, but the other narrators are reliable.

11. Abū Mūsā Al-'Asharī (*raḍiyAllāhu 'anhu*). It is reported by Al-Bazzār, #432—*Kashf*. Haythamī said in *Al-Majma'*, 2/30: In the chain is Muḥammad Ibn 'Abdullāh Ibn 'Umayr Ibn 'Ubayd, and his ḥadīth are rejected.

[82] It is the narration of Abū Umamah (*raḍiyAllāhu 'anhu*).

The prayer (*ṣalah*) is a direct connection (*ṣilah*) between the servant (*ʿabd*) and his Lord (*Rabb*). It is a intimate discourse, which shows its effects on the hearts (*tajalliyah lil-qulūb*) of those that have perception (*ʿārifīn*) and nearness (*qurb*) to Him. Before the prayer, He legislated purification (*ṭahārah*), because it is not befitting to stand (*wuqūf*) in front of Allāh, the Mighty and Majestic, in private conversation (*khalwa*) with Him, except in a pure state (*ṭāḥir*). As for the one who is impure with filth that is visible or otherwise, then it is not appropriate to draw close to Allāh in that manner. Allāh legislated that the worshiper (*musalli*) wash his limbs with water. Through this purification the sins (*ṭahāratul-dhunūb*) are expiated as a result. So for the one that wants to engage in conversation with his Lord, then let them purify themselves both inward and outward, after which He legislated walking to the *masjids*.

Also there is the expiation of sins (*takfīr al-khatāya*) until the purge from sins is complete. If anything remains after *wuḍū*, the servant stands before Allāh after completing purification, both hidden (*bāṭin*) and apparent (*ẓāhir*), until he has no filth or sins left.

For this reason also, He legislated the renewal of repentance (*tajīd al-tawbah*) and seeking forgiveness (*istighfār*) after the end of every wuḍū until the purification from sins is complete as reported by Nasāʾī from the ḥadīth of Abū Saʿīd (*raḍiyAllāhu ʿanhu*) in both Marfūʿ and Mawqūf forms: 'Whoever makes *wuḍū* properly then says once finished:

(سبحانك اللّهُمّ وبحمدك، أستغفرُك وأتوبُ إليك)

> "Glory is to you O Allāh, and praise. I seek forgiveness from you and I turn to you in repentance."

Then it is stamped and placed under the throne (*ʿarsh*) and not unsealed (*khutm*) until the Day of Judgment.'[83]

When a servant strives to perfect his purification (*takmīl al-ṭahārah*) and his walking to the masjid, if it does not wipe away his sins then the prayer completes the expiation of his sins. As (it has been made clear) in the two books of ḥadīth Bukhārī and Muslim on the authority of Abū Hurayrah (*raḍiyAllāhu 'anhu*) from the Prophet (ﷺ) who said: "What do you think of a person that has a river by his door that he bathes in five times a day, would he have dirt left on him?" They said: 'No dirt would be left on him.'

He (ﷺ) said: "Likewise the five prayers wipe away the sins."[84]

So if the *wuḍū* is enough to expiate his sins by itself, then walking to the *masjid* and the prayer after it will be an increase in good deeds (*ziyāda al-ḥasanāt*). This is what was meant in the statement of the Prophet (ﷺ) in the ḥadīth of 'Uthmān (*raḍiyAllāhu 'anhu*) and Al-Sanābihī (*raḍiyAllāhu 'anhu*): "...the walking and his prayer is extra reward." Both ḥadīth have been mentioned previously.

Majority of scholars (have agreed that) all these reasons only expiate minor sins (*ṣighār*) and not major sins (*kibār*). 'Aṭā' and others from the Salaf have deduced this from the *wuḍū*.

Salmān Al-Farisī (*raḍiyAllāhu 'anhu*) said: 'The *wuḍū* expiates the small sins, and walking to the *masjid* expiates more (or greater) than that, and the prayer expiate even more still (or greater).' Reported by Muḥammad Naṣr Al-Marwazī.

[83] Nasā'ī in his *'Amal Yawm wa'l-layl*, #81

[84] Bukhārī, #528 and Muslim, #667.

That which shows major sins are not expiated is (the narration) that is in Bukhārī and Muslim narrated on the authority of Abū Hurayrah (*raḍiyAllāhu ʿanhu*) from the Prophet (ﷺ) who said: "The five daily prayers, the Friday prayer to the next Friday Prayer, and the Ramaḍān to the next Ramaḍān, all expiate sins that occurred in between them, as long as the major sins are avoided."[85]

In Ṣaḥīḥ Muslim, it is narrated on the authority of ʿUthmān (*raḍiyAllāhu ʿanhu*) from the Prophet (ﷺ) who said: "There is no Muslim that attends to the obligatory prayers, perfecting his *wuḍū*, his *khusūʿ*, his bowing and his prostration. Except that it is an expiation for sins that have preceded, as long as major sins are avoided, and that is for all of time."[86]

So look at how easy it is for you to expiate sins. Maybe you will purify yourself from sins before you die and meet it (death) completely purified from sin, and then it would be appropriate that you live in paradise (a place of safety from all evil) near Him. However if you refuse to do so, wanting instead to die upon the impurity of sins, which then will only be purified with the billows of the hellfire.

O you! Don't you know that it is not befitting to draw close to Him except for a person pure of sins? If you wish to be close to Him today then purify your inner and outer self, and if you wish to be close to Him tomorrow, then purify your heart from everything else besides Him so you can be worthy for His nearness:

[85] Muslim, #233, but not in Bukhārī, attributing it to him is an oversight from Ibn Rajab (may Allāh have mercy upon him)

[86] Muslim, #228.

يَوْمَ لَا يَنفَعُ مَالٌ وَلَا بَنُونَ ﴿٨٨﴾ إِلَّا مَنْ أَتَى ٱللَّهَ بِقَلْبٍ سَلِيمٍ ﴿٨٩﴾

"The Day on which neither wealth nor sons will be of any use, except to those who come to Allāh with a sound and flawless heart."

[*al-Shuʿarā* (26): 88-89]

The sound heart (*al-qalb al-salīm*) is the one which has only the love (*maḥabba*) of Allāh in it, and love (*maḥabba*) for what Allāh loves. Indeed Allāh is pure (*ṭayyib*) and He only accepts that which are pure (*ṭayyib*). So not everyone is suited to be a neighbour of Allāh, the Most High tomorrow, nor are they suited to converse with him today (through the prayer), neither is it befitting to converse in every situation:

People are of different kinds,
some treacherous while others honest.
How far off the mark it is to expect from dirt something pure.
Presence is not befitting in front of a crude heart.

CHAPTER FOUR

The Third Reason to Expiate Sins is Sitting in the *Masjids* after the Prayer

What is meant by sitting, is waiting in *masjid* for the next prayer as in the ḥadīth of Abū Hurayrah (*raḍiyAllāhu 'anhu*): "Waiting for a prayer after a prayer, and that is the firm hold, that is the firm hold, that is the firm hold."[87]

So he made this the same as guarding the frontier (*ribāṭ*) in the way of Allāh (*fī sabīlilāh*) the Mighty and Majestic. This is better (*afḍal*) than merely sitting before the prayer to begin, for the one who sits in the masjid waiting to perform the prayer then leave after completing the prayer, shortens his stay. As opposed to the one who prays and then sits waiting for next prayer, then his waiting is longer. Every time one prays a prayer, then sits and waits for the next prayer, spends his whole time in obedience, and that is equal to guarding the frontier in the way of Allāh, the Mighty and Majestic.

In the *Musnad*[88] and *Sunan* Ibn Mājah[89] on the authority of 'Abdullāh Ibn 'Amr (*raḍiyAllāhu 'anhu*) who said: 'We finished

[87] The explanation of this has preceded.

[88] Aḥmad in his *Musnad*, 2/186, 208.

Praying with the Messenger (ﷺ) the Maghrib prayer. Those who wanted to leave, departed and those who wanted stay behind, remained behind.' Then Messenger of Allāh (ﷺ) came out suddenly, grasping for breath and his knees were visible. He said: "Have glad tidings! Your Lord has opened a door from the doors of the heavens boasting about you to the angels, saying: 'Look at my servants they have performed an obligatory prayer and they are waiting for next one.'"

In the *Musnad*, it is reported on the authority of Abū Hurayrah (*raḍiyAllāhu 'anhu*) who narrated from the Prophet (ﷺ) saying: "The person waiting for the next prayer after a prayer is like the knight whose horse is strong in the face of his enemy. The angels of Allāh send salutations upon him as long as he remains in a state of purity and does not leave. That is the greatest form of guarding the frontier."[90]

In the statement: "sitting in the *masjids* after the prayers...." this also covers sitting for the remembrance (of Allāh), reading (*qirā'a*) the Qur'ān, listening to knowledge (*samā' al-'ilm*) and teaching (*ta'līm*) it and so on. Especially after the Morning Prayer (*ṣalat al-ṣubḥa*) until the sunrise. The texts that have been reported show the virtue (*faḍl*) of that. It is similar to the one that sits and waits for the next prayer, because he has performed what he came to the *masjid* to do and now sits and waits for another form of obedience (*ṭā'at*).

[89] Ibn Mājah, #801. Al-Mundhirī said in *al-Targhīb*, 1/282: The narrators are reliable and Abū Ayūb is Al-Marāgī Al-'Atqī is reliable I don't think he heard from 'Abdullāh and Allāh knows best. Būṣāyrī said in *Zawā'id*, 1/102: The narrators are reliable.

[90] Aḥmad in his *Musnad*, 2/352. Al-Mundhirī said in *Al-Targhīb*, 1/284 the chain of narration of Aḥmad is good and Al-Haythamī said in *Al-Majma'*, 2/36: In it is Nafi' Ibn Sulayman Al-Qurashī who is considered reliable by Abū Ḥatim and the remainder of the narrators are narrators of Bukhārī.

It has been reported in Bukhārī that the Prophet (ﷺ) said: "There is no group of people that gather in a house, from the houses of Allāh, the Most High, reciting the book of Allāh, studying it between themselves, except tranquillity descends upon them and mercy envelops them. The angels surround them, and Allāh mentions them to those who are present with Him."[91]

As for the one sitting before the prayer waiting for a specific prayer, then he is (considered) in the prayer until he actually prays. In the Two Ṣaḥīḥs, it is reported on the authority of Anas (*raḍiyAllāhu ʿanhu*) from the Prophet (ﷺ) that when he once delayed the *ʿIsha* prayer very late, so when he came out to pray with them, he said to them: "Indeed you are in the state of prayer as long as you are waiting for the prayer."[92]

Also reported by them, on the authority of Abū Hurayrah (*raḍiyAllāhu ʿanhu*) from the Prophet (ﷺ) who said: "The angels send prayers on anyone of you as long as he is in the place of prayer and remains in a state of purity (*wuḍū*) by saying: 'O Allāh forgive him, O Allāh have mercy upon him.' You continue to be in a state of prayer as long as it is the prayer that keeps you (waiting). Nothing other than the prayer keeps him from going back to his family."[93]

In a narration of Muslim: "As long as he does not harm anyone, and does not break his state of purification."[94]

[91] Muslim, #2699.

[92] Bukhārī, #572 and Muslim. #640.

[93] The reference for this has preceded.

[94] Muslim, #649.

This shows that the meaning of not breaking the state of purification: is what is said on the tongue and so forth by way of harming others. Also it was explained by Abū Hurayrah (*raḍiyAllāhu 'anhu*) as breaking of purification from the private parts, and it has been said to include both.

In the *Musnad*, it has been reported on the authority of 'Uqbah Ibn 'Amir (*raḍiyAllāhu 'anhu*) that the Prophet (ﷺ) said: "The one sitting devoting his time for the prayer is like the devout person. He is written from among the people who are praying from the moment he left his house until he returns."[95]

In another narration of his: "So when he has prayed in the *masjid* and then sits down, he is like the devout fasting person in continuous obedience, until he returns."[96]

There are many narrations with similar meaning.

In summary, sitting in the *masjid* for actions of obedience has great virtue. As reported in the ḥadīth on the authority of Abū Hurayrah (*raḍiyAllāhu 'anhu*) that the Prophet (ﷺ) said: "No Muslim who regularly attend the *masjids* to perform the prayers and remembers Allāh, except that Allāh is pleased with him, just as the family of one who is absent feels happy when he comes back to them."[97]

It has been narrated by Darrāj from Abū'l-Haytham on the au-

[95] Aḥmad, 4/159.

[96] Aḥmad, 4/159.

[97] Aḥmad, 2/328, 453, Ibn Mājah, #800 and Al-Būṣāyrī said in *al-Zawā'id,* 1/102: This chain of narration is authentic.

thority of Abū Sa'īd (*raḍiyAllāhu 'anhu*) from the Prophet (ﷺ) who said: "Whoever loves the *masjid*, Allāh loves him."[98]

Sa'īd Ibn Al-Mūsāyyib said: 'Whoever sits in the *masjids* then (it is like he) is in a gathering with Allāh, the Mighty and Majestic. It has been authentically reported from the Prophet (ﷺ) that he counted of the seven who will shaded by Allāh's shade, on the day there is no shade except His: "A man whose heart is connected to the *masjid*, when he leaves it, he is longing to return back."[99]

Indeed staying in the *masjid* for acts of obedience is a way of expiating sins (*mukaffir lil-dhunūb*) because it requires struggling against one's self (*mujahada al-nafs*). Holding back one's desires, which lean towards going out into the earth seeking sustenance, or enjoying the company of people and conversing with them, or going out for leisure in elegant places and living in nice homes, and other places of recreation. So whoever restrains himself by staying in the *masjid* for acts of obedience, then he is guarding for the sake of Allāh, going against his desires, and that is the best forms of patience (*ṣabr*) and struggle (*jihād*).

This type (of action) i.e. what pains the self and opposes his desires (*hawā*), is an expiation of sins (*kafārat lil-dhunūb*), even though the servant does not have any illness that would expiate his sins (*maraḍ*) and the like. So how would it be for one who goes out of his own way to choose an action in order to draw near to Allāh, the Mighty and Majestic?

[98] Ibn 'Adī, 4/152, and Ṭabarānī in *Al-Awsaṭ*, #6383. Ṭabarānī said: This ḥadīth was not narrated from Darrāj except Ibn Lahi'ah and 'Amr Ibn Khālid exclusively (took from him). Al-Haythamī, 2/23, said: In the chain is Ibn Lahi'ah and there is talk about him.

[99] Bukhārī, #660 and Muslim, #1031.

This type of struggle (*jihād*) in the way of Allāh necessitates the expiation of all sins (*takfir al-dhunūb*).

It is with this meaning precisely that walking is also an expiation of sins, (because) it is also a type of struggle in the way of Allāh, as reported by Ṭabarānī from the ḥadīth of Abū Umāmah (*raḍiyAllāhu 'anhu*) from the Prophet (ﷺ): "Going and coming to the *masjids* is *jihād* in the way of Allāh."[100]

Ziyād, the freed slave of Ibn 'Abbās (*raḍiyAllāhu 'anhumā*), was one of the righteous worshippers (*'ibād al-ṣāliḥīn*). He used to frequent the *masjid* in Medīnah, once he was heard rebuking himself saying: 'Where do you want to go? To somewhere better than this masjid? You want to see the house of such and such?'

The *masjids* on earth are the houses of Allāh, that Allāh has attached to Himself in order to honour (*tashrīf*) them. The hearts of those who love Allāh, the Mighty and Majestic, are connected to them, because they are connected to Him, so they are at ease, frequently visiting them, in order to declare His remembrance inside them:

فِي بُيُوتٍ أَذِنَ ٱللَّهُ أَن تُرْفَعَ
وَيُذْكَرَ فِيهَا ٱسْمُهُۥ يُسَبِّحُ لَهُۥ فِيهَا بِٱلْغُدُوِّ وَٱلْآصَالِ ﴿٣٦﴾
لِلنَّاسِ وَٱللَّهُ بِكُلِّ شَيْءٍ عَلِيمٌ ﴿٣٥﴾ فِي بُيُوتٍ أَذِنَ ٱللَّهُ أَن تُرْفَعَ
وَيُذْكَرَ فِيهَا ٱسْمُهُۥ يُسَبِّحُ لَهُۥ فِيهَا بِٱلْغُدُوِّ وَٱلْآصَالِ ﴿٣٦﴾

[100] In *Al-Mu'jim Al-Kabīr*, 8/7739, and in *Musnad Al-Shāmiyīn*, #879. Haythamī in *Al-Majma'*, 2/29-30, said: In the chain of narration is Al-Qāsim Ibn 'Abdu'l-Raḥmān about whom there is disagreement. Daruquṭunī mentioned in *Al-'Ilal*, 8/141 number #1460 the nature of the disagreement whether it is directly from the Prophet (ﷺ) or not, and said it is better to consider it not directly from the Prophet (ﷺ).

"In the houses [i.e., *masjids*] which Allāh has permitted to be built and in which His name is remembered [i.e., praised]. There are men who proclaim His limitless glory in the morning and the evenings, not distracted by trade or commerce from the remembrance of Allāh and from constancy in prayer and from giving regular charity. They fear a Day when all hearts and eyes will be[fearfully] in turmoil."

[*al-Nūr* (24): 36-37]

Where would those that love (*muḥibbūn*) go if not to the houses of their protector?

The hearts of those who love (*qulūb al-muḥibīn*) are connected to the houses of the one they love, and the steps of the worshippers (*aqdām al-ʿābidīn*) to the houses of the one they worship (*maʿbūd*) are frequent.

O how beautiful is Al-ʿArʿar of Najd and Al-Ban
A sanctuary built by people that is surrounded on all sides
The sweetest of places that the heart yearns for

However eye of the needle is as wide as an open space for the one who has love
Even the sand isn't mentioned except with yearning for the one far away
He has for the ones of sand aims and a place of stay

Longing for Al-ban from the depths of his heart
Not for the sake of Al-ban but those that reside therein

CHAPTER FIVE

The Mention of *'the Ranks'* as reported in the Ḥadīth of Muʿādh (*raḍiyAllāhu ʿanhu*)

There are three types of ranks (*darajāt*):

[5.1 The First Rank is Feeding Others]

The First of these Ranks is: Feeding Others. Allāh has made it one of the reasons (*asbāb*) a person enters Paradise and its bliss. Allāh, the Mighty and the Majestic said:

وَيُطْعِمُونَ ٱلطَّعَامَ عَلَىٰ حُبِّهِۦ مِسْكِينًا
وَيَتِيمًا وَأَسِيرًا ﴿٨﴾ إِنَّمَا نُطْعِمُكُمْ لِوَجْهِ ٱللَّهِ لَا نُرِيدُ مِنكُمْ جَزَآءً وَلَا شُكُورًا
﴿٩﴾ إِنَّا نَخَافُ مِن رَّبِّنَا يَوْمًا عَبُوسًا قَمْطَرِيرًا ﴿١٠﴾ فَوَقَىٰهُمُ ٱللَّهُ شَرَّ ذَٰلِكَ
ٱلْيَوْمِ وَلَقَّىٰهُمْ نَضْرَةً وَسُرُورًا ﴿١١﴾ وَجَزَىٰهُم بِمَا صَبَرُوا۟ جَنَّةً وَحَرِيرًا
﴿١٢﴾ مُّتَّكِـِٔينَ فِيهَا عَلَى ٱلْأَرَآئِكِ لَا يَرَوْنَ فِيهَا شَمْسًا وَلَا زَمْهَرِيرًا ﴿١٣﴾
وَدَانِيَةً عَلَيْهِمْ ظِلَٰلُهَا وَذُلِّلَتْ قُطُوفُهَا تَذْلِيلًا ﴿١٤﴾ وَيُطَافُ عَلَيْهِم بِـَٔانِيَةٍ
مِّن فِضَّةٍ وَأَكْوَابٍ كَانَتْ قَوَارِيرَا۠ ﴿١٥﴾ قَوَارِيرَا۟ مِن فِضَّةٍ قَدَّرُوهَا تَقْدِيرًا ﴿١٦﴾
وَيُسْقَوْنَ فِيهَا كَأْسًا كَانَ مِزَاجُهَا زَنجَبِيلًا ﴿١٧﴾ عَيْنًا فِيهَا تُسَمَّىٰ سَلْسَبِيلًا

﴿١٨﴾ ۞ وَيَطُوفُ عَلَيْهِمْ وِلْدَٰنٌ مُّخَلَّدُونَ إِذَا رَأَيْتَهُمْ حَسِبْتَهُمْ لُؤْلُؤًا مَّنثُورًا
﴿١٩﴾ وَإِذَا رَأَيْتَ ثَمَّ رَأَيْتَ نَعِيمًا وَمُلْكًا كَبِيرًا ﴿٢٠﴾ عَٰلِيَهُمْ ثِيَابُ سُندُسٍ
خُضْرٌ وَإِسْتَبْرَقٌ وَحُلُّوٓا أَسَاوِرَ مِن فِضَّةٍ وَسَقَىٰهُمْ رَبُّهُمْ شَرَابًا
طَهُورًا ﴿٢١﴾

"They give food, despite their love for it to the poor, and the orphans and the prisoner. [Saying], 'We feed you only out of desire for the countenance [i.e., approval] of Allāh alone. We do not want any repayment from you, nor any thanks. Indeed, We fear from our Lord of a distressful and a fateful Day!' So Allāh has safeguarded them from the evil of that Day and has made them find brightness and pure joy. And will reward them for their steadfastness in adversity with a garden [in Paradise] and silk [garments]. [They will be] reclining in it on couches. They will not see therein any [heat of the] sun nor sever cold. Its shading branches will droop down low over them, its ripe fruit hanging down ready to be picked. Vessels of silver and goblets of pure crystal are brought round among them, crystalline [Clear glasses] made from silver they [themselves] have measured them very exactly [of their needs]. They will be given there in a cup to drink mixed with ginger (*zanjabīl*). In it there is a flowing spring called named *salsabīl.* Ageless youths will circulate among them, serving them. Seeing them, you would think them [as beautiful as] scattered pearls. When you look there [in Paradise], you will see delight and a great kingdom. They will wear green garments of fine silk and rich brocade. They will be adorned with silver bracelets. And their Lord will give them a

drink most pure."

[*al-Insān* (76): 8-21]

So He described the fruits and drinks as a reward for them feeding others.

It is reported in Tirmidhī from the ḥadīth of Abū Sa'īd Al-Khudrī (*raḍiyAllāhu 'anhu*) from the Prophet (ﷺ) who said: "Any believer that feeds another believer despite of his own hunger, Allāh will feed him from the fruits of Paradise. And whoever quenches the thirst of a believer dispite his thirst, Allāh will give him a drink from the Sealed Nectar."[101]

In the *Musnad* (of Imām Aḥmad Ibn Ḥanbal)[102] and Tirmidhī[103] it has been reported that the Prophet (ﷺ) said: "Indeed in Paradise are lofty rooms that the outside can be seen from the inside, and the inside from the outside." They said: 'For whom O Messenger of Allāh?' He said: "For the one who feeds others, has pleasant speech, and prays during the night while people are sleeping."

In the ḥadīth of 'Abdullāh Ibn Salām (*raḍiyAllāhu 'anhu*), which has been reported by the People of the *Sunan*, (he said) that he

[101] Tirmidhī, #2449. Tirmidhī said: This ḥadīth is gharīb (strange), this ḥadīth was narrated by 'Attiyah from Abū Sa'īd as mawqūf, and he is more authentic with us and most similar. Abū Ḥātim asked his son in *'Ilal*, 2/171 number #2007 about this ḥadīth and he said: Authentic Mawqūf, the memorisers are not aware of it. Reported by Abū Dāwūd, #1682 from another chain of narrations from Abū Sa'īd (*raḍiyAllāhu 'anhu*).

[102] Reported by 'Abdullāh Ibn Aḥmad in his *Zawā'id*, 1/155-156.

[103] Tirmidhī, #1984, #2527 and said: ḥadīth gharīb (strange), some of the people of knowledge have spoken about 'Abdu'l-Raḥmān Ibn Ishāq due to his memory.

heard when the Prophet (ﷺ) first came to Madīnah saying: "O people spread *salām*, feed others, keep the ties of kinship, pray in the night while people are asleep and you will enter Paradise in peace." [104]

In the ḥadīth reported on the authority of 'Ubadah [Ibn Sāmmit] (*raḍiyAllāhu 'anhu*) from the Prophet (ﷺ) when he was asked: 'What actions are the best?' He (ﷺ) said: "Belief in Allāh, struggling in the way of Allāh, an accepted pilgrimage, and that which is easier than that: feeding others, and having soft speech. Reported by Imām Aḥmad."[105]

In the narration of Ḥānī' Ibn Yazīd (*raḍiyAllāhu 'anhu*) who reported that a man said: 'O Messenger of Allāh show me an action that will enter me into Paradise and keep me far away from the fire?' He (ﷺ) said: "Feed others, and spread greetings of peace (*salām*)."[106]

In the ḥadīth of Hudayfah [Ibn Yaman] (*raḍiyAllāhu 'anhu*) as reported from the Prophet (ﷺ) who said: "Whoevers final action

---

[104] Dārimī, #1468, #2635, Tirmidhī, #2485, Ibn Mājah, #1334, #3251. Tirmidhī said: This ḥadīth is authentic.

[105] This is not in the *Musnad*, rather it is in Ṭabarānī as well as in *Majma' al-Zawā'id* of Haythamī, 5/278-289 where he mentioned it and said: Narrated by Ṭabarānī with two chains of narrations, one of them: Ibn Lahi'ah, and his narrations are good as well as having weakness. The other chain is Suwayd Ibn Ibrāhīm whom Ibn Ma'īn held as reliable in two narrations while Nasā'ī held it as weak, and the rest of the narrators are reliable.

[106] Bukhārī in *Adab ul-Mufrad*, #811, and in *Khalq Af'āl 'Ibād* (page 68), and Al-Bazzār, #2889—*Kashf*, and Ṭabarānī in *Al-Kabīr*, 22/467, 468. Haythamī said in *Majma'*, 5/17: Narrated by Ṭabarānī with two chains of narrators, one of those chains have reliable narrators.

is feeding a needy person will enter Paradise."[107]

Furthermore, in the both Bukhārī and Muslim from the narration of 'Abdullāh Ibn 'Amr (*raḍiyAllāhu 'anhuma*) who reported that a man said: 'O Messenger of Allāh, which is the best Islām?' He (ﷺ) said: "Feeding others, and giving the greetings of peace to those that you know and those that you don't know." [108]

In the narration of Suhayb (*raḍiyAllāhu 'anhu*) that the Prophet (ﷺ) said: "The best of you is the one that feeds others." Reported by Imām Aḥmad.[109]

So feeding others necessitates Paradise (*jannah*), and takes a person away from the fire (*nār*) and saves them from it. Allāh, the Most High says:

فَلَا ٱقْتَحَمَ ٱلْعَقَبَةَ ﴿١١﴾ وَمَآ أَدْرَىٰكَ مَا ٱلْعَقَبَةُ ﴿١٢﴾
فَكُّ رَقَبَةٍ ﴿١٣﴾ أَوْ إِطْعَٰمٌ فِى يَوْمٍ ذِى مَسْغَبَةٍ ﴿١٤﴾ يَتِيمًا ذَا مَقْرَبَةٍ
﴿١٥﴾ أَوْ مِسْكِينًا ذَا مَتْرَبَةٍ ﴿١٦﴾

"But he has not broken through the difficult pass. And what can make you know what is [breaking through] the difficult pass? It is the freeing of a slave. Or feeding on a day of severe hunger. An orphan of near relationship. Or a needy person in misery."

[*Balad* (90): 11-16]

107 Abū Nu'aym in *Akhbār Asbahān*, 1/218-219, and there is a break in the chain.

108 Bukhārī, #12 and Muslim, #39.

109 Aḥmad in his *Musnad*, 5/16 and Haythamī said in *Al-Majma'*, 5/17: Narrated by Aḥmad, and in the chain is 'Abdullāh Ibn Muḥammad Ibn 'Aqīl, and his narrations are good with some weakness. The rest of the narrators are reliable.

In a ḥadīth of Bukhārī from the Prophet (ﷺ) (it mentions that he) said: "Fear the fire even it be with a part of a date."[110]

Abū Mūsā Al-'Asharī (*raḍiyAllāhu 'anhu*) said to his son: 'Remember the story of the man with a the loaf of bread.' Then he narrated that a man from the children of Israel devoted his entire life to worshiping Allāh for seventy years. One day the devil made an attractive woman seduce him and enticed him to stay with her for seven days. When he left the house of the women [ashamed of himself and repentant], on the way he ended up staying with some poor men. He gave them a loaf of bread that they wanted, instead of having it himself and died shortly after. When his deeds were weighed, the seventy years of worship he offered did not amount up to the weight of the sins he committed during the last seven days [the sins surpassed his good deeds]. Then the loaf of bread was weighed against the last seven days he stayed with the woman and the deed of giving a single loaf of bread to the needy outweighed the seven days [of sins].[111]

Feeding others is emphasised more for the hungry and the neighbours more specifically. As in a narration in Bukhārī[112] from the ḥadīth of Abū Mūsā Al-'Ash'arī (*raḍiyAllāhu 'anhu*) from the Prophet (ﷺ) who said: "Feed the hungry, and visit the sick and free the one suffering."[113]

[110] Bukhārī, #6540 and Muslim, #1016.

[111] Abū Nu'aym in *al-Ḥilyah*, 1/263 in full.

[112] Bukhārī, #3046.

[113] The captive, and anyone that is made to be humbled or surrender are regarded as suffering. *Al-Nihayah*, 3/314

Also in Muslim is a narration reported on the authority of Abū Dharr (*raḍiyAllāhu 'anhu*) that the Prophet (ﷺ) said to him: "O Abū Dharr! When you cook increase the amount of water you use and share it with your neighbour."[114]

In the *Musnad*[115] and Ṣaḥīḥ Al-Ḥākim[116] it was reported on the authority of Ibn 'Umar (*raḍiyAllāhu 'anhumā*) from the Prophet (ﷺ) who said: "Any people that own land in which a person goes hungry in, then Allāh, the Mighty and Majestic removes His protection from them."

The Prophet (ﷺ) said: "No believer is ever relieved of hunger without his neighbour (also being satisfied)."[117]

In the Ṣaḥīḥ of Al-Ḥākim it is reported on the authority of Ibn 'Abbās (*raḍiyAllāhu 'anhumā*) from the Prophet (ﷺ) who said: "He is not a believer, the one who goes to sleep on a full stomach, while

[114] Muslim, #2625.

[115] Aḥmad in his *Musnad*, 2/33 on the authority of Ibn 'Umar (*raḍiyAllāhu 'anhumā*).

[116] Ḥākim, 2/11-12 on the authority of Ibn 'Umar (*raḍiyAllāhu 'anhumā*).
Abū Ḥātim was asked, as mentioned in *Al-'Ilal* of his son, 1/392 about this ḥadīth to which he said: This ḥadīth is munkar (rejected). Ibn Al-Jawzī has placed this among the fabricated narrations.

[117] Aḥmad in his *Musnad*, 1/54, Abū Nu'aym in *al-Ḥilyah*, 9/27 with the wording: *'A man'* instead of believer. Abū Nu'aym said: This ḥadīth is strange, we have written it except from the ḥadīth of 'Umar Ibn Al-Khaṭṭāb (*raḍiyAllāhu 'anhu*) except from this chain of narration, 'Abdu'l-Raḥmān is alone (in narrating it). Haythamī said in *Al-Majma'*, 8/167-168: It was narrated by Aḥmad and Abū Ya'la in part, and the narrators are of Bukhārī except 'Abayah Ibn Rifah'ah who did not hear from 'Umar (*raḍiyAllāhu 'anhu*).

his neighbour goes hungry."[118]

In another narration: "The one who sleeps fully satisfied while his neighbour sleeps hungry has not believed."[119]

So the most virtuous types of generosity, is giving preference to other over yourself, at time when you are in need yourself. As described by Allāh, the Most High concerning the Anṣār (*raḍiyAllāhu 'anhum*) when He said:

وَيُؤْثِرُونَ عَلَىٰٓ أَنفُسِهِمْ وَلَوْ كَانَ بِهِمْ خَصَاصَةٌ

"And they gave them preference over themselves, even though they themselves are needy."

[*al-Ḥashr* (59): 9]

It has been authentically reported[120] that the reason this verse was revealed about a man from the Anṣār (*raḍiyAllāhu 'anhum*) is because he took a guest on request from the Prophet (ﷺ) to host. When the host did not find anything to serve his guest except the food of his children. Therefore he and his wife acted as if they were cooking until their children fell asleep. Then he stood up giving the guest an impression that he is adjusting the light but instead switched it off. He then sat down with his guest and pretended to eat so that the guest would eat with him, all the while he did not

[118] Ḥākim, 4/167. Ḥākim said: This ḥadīth has an authentic chain of narration although not reported the Two Ṣaḥīḥs of Bukhārī and Muslim.

[119] Ṭabarānī reported it in *Al-Kabīr*, 1/751 with something similar. Haythamī said in *Al-Majma'*, 8/167: Reported by Ṭabarānī and Bazzār with the chain of Bazzār being good.

[120] Bukhārī, #3798 and Muslim, #2054 on the authority of Abū Hurayrah (*raḍiyAllāhu 'anhu*).

eat. The next morning he went to the Messenger of Allāh ﷺ) who said to him: "Allāh was amazed at you and your wife, for what you both did last night." Then previous verse was revealed.

Many of the pious predecessors (*salaf*) gave preference to others with their food over themselves while they were fasting or would start to fast, from them: 'Abdullāh Ibn 'Umar; (*raḍiyAllāhu 'anhumā*), and Dāwūd al-Tā'i; 'Abdu'l-'Aziz Ibn Sulaymān; Mālik Ibn Dinār; Aḥmad Ibn Ḥanbal and others.

Ibn 'Umar (*raḍiyAllāhu 'anhumā*) used to only eat with orphans and poor people, and if he realised that his family turned them away he would not eat that night.

Among them were some who would not eat except with a guest. Abū'l-Sawwār Al-'Adawī said: 'The men of the tribe of 'Adī use to pray in this *masjid*, they would never eat alone, so either they found someone to eat with them at home, or they would bring the food with them to the *masjid* and eat with the people there.'

Some of them would feed their brethren while they themselves were fasting. They would sit with them serving and entertaining them. Most notably from them were Al-Ḥasan [al-Baṣrī] and ['Abdullāh] Ibn Al-Mubārak. Ibn Al-Mubārak would only make something he wanted if there was a guest to eat it with him.

Many of them would prefer to feed others over giving charity to the poor and needy. The essence of this has been narrated from Anas (*raḍiyAllāhu 'anhu*) with a weak chain of narration, especially if their tribesmen were not able to find that type of food.

There were some amongst them that would make fine food and

then feed them to the poor among their clan, and say: 'They don't have anything.' Others would say: 'It was not for my own desire that I made it, rather I made it for you.' Whereas others would take a sweet dish and feed the insane person. So their family would say: 'This person doesn't even know (what's going on).' So he would reply: 'But Allāh does.'

Al-Rabīʿ Ibn Khaytham craved for something sweet (*ḥalāwa*) so it was prepared for him, he called some poor people and they ate it. His family mentioned to him how he made them toil to make it, yet he did not eat any of it. (He replied) 'Who besides me ate it?' (i.e. it is the same whether I eat it or they eat.)

Another person said (when something similar happened to him): if I eat then it disappears, whereas if I feed it to someone else then it is preserved with Allāh.

It has been narrated on the authority of ʿAlī (*raḍiyAllāhu ʿanhu*) that he said: 'It is more beloved to me that I call a group of tribesmen to share food, than enter your marketplace and buy a slave and then set him free.'

It is reported from Abū Jaʿfar Muḥammad Ibn ʿAlī who said: 'To call ten people from my brethren to share some food is more beloved to me than freeing ten people from the progeny of Ismaʿīl.'

Should I then proceed to describe to you giving preference to others over oneself to the one that is miserly in performing his obligatory duties? Should I seek bravery from one who is a coward, and seek witness of the new moon from the one considered blind? How great the divide between those who it is said about them:

فَلَمَّآ ءَاتَىٰهُم مِّن فَضْلِهِۦ بَخِلُوا۟ بِهِۦ

"When He does give them from His bounty, they become stingy with it."

[*al-Tawbah* (9): 76]

And between those about whom it is said:

وَيُؤْثِرُونَ عَلَىٰٓ أَنفُسِهِمْ وَلَوْ كَانَ بِهِمْ خَصَاصَةٌ

"And they gave them preference over themselves, even though they themselves are needy."

[*al-Ḥashr* (59): 9]

The difference between them is like those that are awake compared to those that are asleep.

Do not put forward our mention while mentioning them
Not alike is the able bodied when he goes forth compared to the one sitting

So you who wishes to reach the lofty ranks (*'ulu al-darajāt*) without doing righteous actions (*'amal ṣāliḥ*), how far of you are from reaching your goal.

أَمْ حَسِبَ ٱلَّذِينَ ٱجْتَرَحُوا۟ ٱلسَّيِّـَٔاتِ أَن نَّجْعَلَهُمْ كَٱلَّذِينَ
ءَامَنُوا۟ وَعَمِلُوا۟ ٱلصَّٰلِحَٰتِ سَوَآءً مَّحْيَاهُمْ وَمَمَاتُهُمْ ۚ سَآءَ
مَا يَحْكُمُونَ ﴿٢١﴾

"Or do those who commit evils think that We shall hold them equal with those who have believed and do righteous good deeds so that their lives and deaths will be the same? How bad, indeed, is their judgement!."

[*al-Jāthiyah* (45): 21]

They descended upon Makkah among the tribes of Hashim
While I descended upon Baidā' at the farthest abode

[5.2 The Second Rank is Soft Speech]

The second of these ranks is: Soft speech (*layn al-kalām*) as in the narration: 'To spread the greeting' (*ifshā' al-salām*) which is included in the meaning of soft speech. Allāh, the Mighty and Majestic has said:

وَقُولُوا۟ لِلنَّاسِ حُسْنًا

"And speak good words to people."

[*al-Baqarah* (2): 83]

Allāh, the Most High says:

وَقُل لِّعِبَادِى يَقُولُوا۟ ٱلَّتِى هِىَ أَحْسَنُ

"And say to My servants that they should only speak that which is best."

[*al-Isrā'* (17): 53]

He also said:

ٱدْفَعْ بِٱلَّتِى هِىَ أَحْسَنُ فَإِذَا ٱلَّذِى بَيْنَكَ وَبَيْنَهُۥ عَدَٰوَةٌ كَأَنَّهُۥ
وَلِىٌّ حَمِيمٌ ﴿٣٤﴾ وَمَا يُلَقَّىٰهَآ إِلَّا ٱلَّذِينَ صَبَرُوا۟ وَمَا يُلَقَّىٰهَآ
إِلَّا ذُو حَظٍّ عَظِيمٍ ﴿٣٥﴾

"Repel the bad with something better; and if there is enmity between you and someone else, he may become like a true friend. But none will obtain [the above quality] except those who are truly patient and have self-restraint. None will obtain it but those who have a great portion [of good]."

[*Fuṣṣilat* (41): 34-35]

He the Most High says:

وَجَٰدِلْهُم بِٱلَّتِى هِىَ أَحْسَنُ

"And argue with them in the most kindly manner."
[*al-Naḥl* (16): 125]

And He the Most High said:

۞ وَلَا تُجَٰدِلُوٓا۟ أَهْلَ ٱلْكِتَٰبِ إِلَّا بِٱلَّتِى هِىَ أَحْسَنُ إِلَّا ٱلَّذِينَ ظَلَمُوا۟ مِنْهُمْ

"And only argue with the People of the Scripture in the most kindly manner, except for those who commit injustice among them."
[*al-'Ankabūt* (29): 46]

When the Prophet (ﷺ) said: "The Accepted *Ḥajj* (*ḥajj al-mabrūr*) has no reward for it except Paradise." They said: 'And what is the Accepted *Ḥajj* O Messenger of Allāh?' He (ﷺ) replied: "Feeding others and having soft speech." Reported by Imām Aḥmad[121]

Many other ḥadīth have been mentioned previously regarding feeding others and good speech (*ṭayyib al-kalam*).

In an authentic ḥadīth from the Prophet (ﷺ) who said: "The good word (*al-kalima al-ṭayyiba*) is charity."[122]

Also: "Fear the fire even it be with part of a date, and whoever

[121] Aḥmad in his *Musnad*, 3/325,334 on the authority of Jābir Ibn 'Abdullāh (*raḍiyAllāhu 'anhu*). Al-Ḥāfiẓ said in *Al-Fatḥ*, 3/382: There is a weakness in the chain. A part of the first ḥadīth is in the both Bukhārī and Muslim from the narration of Abū Hurayrah (*raḍiyAllāhu 'anhu*).

[122] A part of a ḥadīth reported by Bukhārī, #2989 and Muslim, 2/699 on the authority of Abū Hurayrah (*raḍiyAllāhu 'anhu*).

does not find (even that) then with a good word (*kalima ṭayyiba*)."[123]

As for those who spread the greetings of the salām, it necessitates a persons entry into Paradise. In the narration of Muslim reported on the authority of Abū Hurayrah (*raḍiyAllāhu ʿanhu*) that the Prophet (ﷺ) said: "By the One in whose hands my soul is in, none of you will enter Paradise until you believe, and none of you will believe until you love one another. Shall I not inform you of something that if you do it you will love one another? Spread *salām* amongst yourselves."[124]

Abū Dāwūd reported the ḥadīth of Abū Umāmah (*raḍiyAllāhu ʿanhu*) from the Prophet (ﷺ) who said: "Indeed the most worthy of people with Allāh are those that initiate *salām*."[125]

Ibn Masʿūd (*raḍiyAllāhu ʿanhu*) narrated directly from the Prophet (ﷺ) in Marfūʿ and in Mawqūf[126] form: "When a man passes by a group of people and gives them the greeting of *salām* and they respond to him, then he has a rank over them because he gave them *salām* (first). And if they do not respond then a gathering better and more pure respond to him (instead)."[127]

It has been narrated on the authority of ʿImrān Ibn Ḥusayn

[123] Bukhārī, #6023 and Muslim, #1016.

[124] Muslim, #54.

[125] Abū Dāwūd, #5197.

[126] Bukhārī in *Al-Adab*, #1039. Al-Ḥāfiẓ Ibn Ḥajr said in *Al-Fatḥ*, 11/13: The path of the mawqūf narration is stronger.

[127] Bazzār, #1999—*Kashf* and Ṭabarānī in *Al-Kabīr*, 10/9800. Bazzār said: More than one person has narrated it in mawqūf form. Haythamī said in *Al-Majma*

(*raḍiyAllāhu 'anhu*) and others that a man entered into the presence of the Prophet (ﷺ) and said: 'Peace (*salām*) be upon you ['*assalāmu alaykum*].' So the Prophet (ﷺ) said: "Ten." Then another person came and said: 'Peace be upon you and Allāh's mercy ['*assalāmu alaykum wa-raḥamatullāhi*].' So the Prophet (ﷺ) said: "Twenty." Then another man came and said: 'Peace be upon you and the mercy of Allāh and His blessings ['*assalāmu alaykum wa-raḥamatullāhi wa-barakatuhu*].' So the Messenger of Allāh (ﷺ) said: "Thirty." Reported by Tirmidhī[128] and others.[129]

It has been transmitted by Abū Dāwūd.[130] And he added: 'Then another person came and said: 'Peace be upon you; and Allāh's mercy; and His blessings; and His forgiveness ['*assalāmu alaykum wa-raḥamatullāhi wa-barakatuhu wa-maghfiratu*].' The Prophet (ﷺ) said: "Forty." Then he said: "This is how the virtues are."[131]

This narration has already preceded that: "To give *salām* to those that you know and don't know."

[It is mentioned] in the narration of Ibn Mas'ūd (*raḍiyAllāhu 'anhu*) directly from the Prophet (ﷺ) that: "From the signs of the

8/29: It was narrated by Bazzār with two chains, and Ṭabarānī with many chains, one of which the chain of narrators are narrators of Bukhārī as is held by Bazzār and Ṭabarānī.

[128] Tirmidhī, #2689 and he said (the ḥadīth is) ḥasan ṣaḥīḥ.

[129] Aḥmad in his *Musnad*, 4/439-440, Dārimī, 2/277-278 and Nasā'ī in *'Amal Al-Yaum wa'l-Layl*, #337.

[130] Abū Dāwūd, #5190.

[131] This addition has been reported by Abū Dāwūd, #5196 and Al-Ḥāfiẓ said in *Al-Fatḥ*, 11/6: Its chain is weak.

hour is that man would only give *salām* to the person that he knew." Reported by Imām Aḥmad.[132]

The virtues of feeding others and speaking gently have been brought together in order to perfect righteousness (*iḥsān*) towards the creation in speech (*qawl*) and action (*'aml*). So this kindness is not complete by just feeding others only, rather with soft speech and spreading *salām*. If someone is not gentle in their speech then their kindness in actions such as feeding others is void. Allāh, the Most High says:

يَٰٓأَيُّهَا
ٱلَّذِينَ ءَامَنُوا۟ لَا تُبْطِلُوا۟ صَدَقَٰتِكُم بِٱلْمَنِّ وَٱلْأَذَىٰ

"O you who have believed! Do not invalidate your charitable deeds with demands for gratitude or hurting [the feelings of others]."

[*al-Baqarah* (2): 264]

It may be that dealing with people with good speech (*qawl ḥasan*) is more beloved to them than giving them wealth as Luqmān (*'alayhis-salām*) said to his son: 'O my son! Let your speech be good, and your face be cheerful, this will be more beloved to the people than if you gave them gold and silver.'[133]

The Prophet (ﷺ) used to be soft in speech to those that were evil (*sharr*) towards him, that would negate their evil. He (ﷺ) would not confront anyone with an expression on his face that they would not like, nor was he lewd or indecent.

[132] Aḥmad in his *Musnad*, 1/387, 405, 406.

[133] Please see the published work '*The Wise Counsel of Luqmān*.' Published by Dār as-Sunnah Publishers, Birmingham, UK, 1st ed., 2016. This work contains many beneficial instructions and counsels found in the story of Luqmān.

It has been narrated on the authority of Ibn 'Umar (*radiyAllāhu 'anhumā*) that he would often say:

O my son righteousness is something easy
A cheerful face and soft speech.
Others would say:
Take hold of pardon and order with good as
You have been commanded and turn away from the ignorant.
And soften your speech to all of creation
For softness from those of high stature is commendable.

Allāh, the Mighty and Majestic has described in His book the inhabitants of Paradise (*ahlu'l-jannah*) as people that treated the creation with generosity (*iḥsān*) using their wealth and bearing harm from them, as He says:

﴿ وَسَارِعُوٓا۟ إِلَىٰ مَغْفِرَةٍ مِّن رَّبِّكُمْ وَجَنَّةٍ عَرْضُهَا
ٱلسَّمَـٰوَٰتُ وَٱلْأَرْضُ أُعِدَّتْ لِلْمُتَّقِينَ ﴿١٣٣﴾ ٱلَّذِينَ يُنفِقُونَ
فِى ٱلسَّرَّآءِ وَٱلضَّرَّآءِ وَٱلْكَـٰظِمِينَ ٱلْغَيْظَ وَٱلْعَافِينَ
عَنِ ٱلنَّاسِ ۗ وَٱللَّهُ يُحِبُّ ٱلْمُحْسِنِينَ ﴿١٣٤﴾

"And race one another for forgiveness from your Lord and a Garden [i.e., Paradise] as vast as the heavens and earth, prepared for the righteous. Those who spend [in the cause of Allāh] in times of ease and hardship, who control their anger and who pardon other people - Allāh loves the doers of good."

[*Āl-'Imrān* (3): 133-134]

So spending in prosperity (*sarrā'*) and adversity (*darrā'*) necessitates the utmost degree of kindness (*iḥsān*), whether it be a lot or a little. Meanwhile to hide ones anger (*ghayẓ*) and pardon (*'afū*) mankind requires the need to not deal with people in the same evil way as they may have done, both in action or speech. All of this implies softening the speech, while avoiding lewdness *(faḥsh)* or harshness *(ighlāẓ)* even if it is allowed. This is the highest level of kindness, for this reason the Most High says:

وَٱللَّهُ يُحِبُّ ٱلْمُحْسِنِينَ ﴿١٣٤﴾

"Allāh loves the doers of good"

[*Āl-'Imrān* (3): 134]

From this (verse) is the statement of some whilst being asked about good manners (*ḥusn al-khuluq*), so one of them said: 'Being open handed with *nada*[134] and withholding of harm. This description is mentioned in the Qur'ān in a more comprehensive way, because it describes them as bestowing generously and bearing the harm from others with patience.'

With good manners (*ḥusn al-khuluq*), the servant (*'abd*) may reach levels (*darajāt*) of those who exert much effort (*mujtahidūn*) in worship (*'ibādah*), as Prophet (ﷺ) said: "A person with his good manners, may reach a level of a person who constantly fasts during the day and stands (in prayer) during the night"[135]

One of the Salaf was seen in a dream. So he was asked about some of his righteous brethren to which he said: 'He was raised in Paradise due to this good manners.'

[134] *Al-Nada*: Generosity and kindness. *Lisanul 'Arab*,15/315

[135] Abū Dāwūd, #4798 and others. In the chain is Irsal between Al-Muṭṭalib Ibn Hantab and 'Ā'ishah (*raḍiyAllāhu 'anhā*). Reported by Bukhārī in *Adabul Mufrad*, #284 and others on the authority of Abū Hurayrah (*raḍiyAllāhu 'anhu*). Also reported by Ṭabarānī in *Al-Awsaṭ*, #6273 on the authority of 'Alī (*raḍiyAllāhu 'anhu*) and he said: No one besides Isma'īl Ibn 'Ayyash narrates this on the authority of 'Alī (*raḍiyAllāhu 'anhu*).

Furthermore, soft speech (*ilāna al-qawl*) is recommended for enjoining the good (*amr b'il-ma'rūf*) and forbidding the evil (*nahyi al-munkar*). It should be done with gentleness (*rifq*) as the Most High says regarding the disbelievers:

$$\text{وَجَٰدِلْهُم بِٱلَّتِى هِىَ أَحْسَنُ}$$

"And argue with them in the most kindly manner."
[*al-Naḥl* (16): 125]

One of the Salaf said: 'You will never cause someone to be angry with you, except they will not accept anything from you.'

The companions of Ibn Mas'ūd (*raḍiyAllāhu 'anhu*) use to say to people when they saw them doing something disliked: 'Take it easy, may Allāh bless you.'

One of the *tābi'īn*[136] saw a man standing with a woman so he said to them both: 'Indeed Allāh sees you both, may Allāh cover us and you.'

Al-Ḥasan was called to share some food. A silver container was brought that had a sweet dish in it, so he took out the food and put it on his bread and ate from it. Some of those present said: 'This is forbidding the evil in silence.'

Fuḍayl Ibn 'Iyāḍ saw a man fiddling around in his prayer so he restrained him roughly. The man said to him: 'O you! Who instructs good for Allāh's sake you ought be gentle.' So Fuḍayl cried and said: 'You are right.'

---

[136] A companion of the Companions of the Prophet

Shu'ayb Ibn Harb said: 'Sufyān Al-Thawrī would pass by a gathering of people playing chess and he would ask: 'What are you doing?' It would be said to him: 'O father of 'Abdullāh they looking at a book.' So he would lower his head and keep walking showing that he was displeased with what they were actually doing.'

Sufyān said: 'No one enjoins the good or forbids the evil except one who possesses three characteristics: being gentle (*rafiq*) with what he enjoins, and gentle (*rafiq*) when he forbids something. Also being just (*'adl*) when he enjoins the good and forbids the evil. All the while having knowledge (*'ilm*) of both what he is enjoining and forbidding.'

Imām Aḥmad said: 'People are in need of humouring (*mudārā*) and gentleness (*rifq*) when it comes to enjoining good and forbidding evil, except for a man who is openly flagrant (*ghilẓa*) in sinning (*fisq*) then he has no sanctity (*ḥurma*).'

Many of the Salaf would enjoin the good and prevent people from vices in secret (*sirr*).

Umm Dardā' said: 'Whoever admonishes his brother in secret (*sirr*) has beautified him, and whosoever does so openly (*'alaniya*) has disgraced him.'

Likewise, confronting hurtful words with soft speech. Allāh says:

ٱدۡفَعۡ بِٱلَّتِي هِيَ أَحۡسَنُ

"Repel the evil deed with something that is better."

[*Fuṣṣilat* (41): 34]

And He the Most High says:

وَيَدْرَءُونَ بِٱلْحَسَنَةِ ٱلسَّيِّئَةَ أُوْلَٰٓئِكَ لَهُمْ عُقْبَى ٱلدَّارِ ﴿٢٢﴾

"And prevent evil with good—it is they who will have the Ultimate Abode."

[*al-Ra'd* (13): 22]

Some of the Salaf said: 'The man would revile another man (for some reason) so he would say back to him: 'If you are truthful in what you say then may Allāh forgive me, and if you are untruthful then may Allāh forgive you.''

Once on a journey Salim Ibn 'Abdullāh's riding beast clashed with another mans. So the man said to him: 'I see you as an evil man!' Salim in reply said to him: 'I don't see you trying to keep away!'

A woman said to Mālik Ibn Dinār: 'You are show off.' He said: 'When did you come to know my name?' No one else but you know me from the people of Baṣrah (meaning you might be right).

Some of them passed by a group of children playing with coconuts, they tread on some of them and cracked them unintentionally, so one of the children said to him: 'O Shaikh of the fire (out of anger).' So the Shaikh sat down and wept saying: 'No one else but he knows me.'

Others passed by some people with their companions along the path and ash was thrown on them. So the Shaikh said to his companions: 'Whoever deserves the fire let him reconcile himself with the ash (i.e. free yourself from doing wrong), if he wants to be a winner.'

A solider saw Ibrāhīm Ibn Adham outside town and so he asked about the civilization there, so he pointed to the graves, then hit his head and carried on. Then it was told to the solider that is Ibrāhīm Ibn Adham. So he went back to him and apologised so Ibrāhīm said to him: 'A head that needs an apology I have left in Balakh (A place in Afghanistan).'

Another solider passed by him while he was looking at a garden belonging to a group of people for rent. So he asked him if he could take something but he never did and said: 'The people of this garden have not given us permission.' He then hit his head and starting to shake his head while saying I will hit a head as long as it disobeys Allāh.[137]

[5.3. The Third Ranks is Praying at Night]

The third of these ranks: Praying at night (*ṣalat bi'l-layl*) while people are sleeping. The night prayer is something that will necessitate (*mujibāt*) Paradise as mentioned before in more than one ḥadīth.

The statement of Allāh, the Mighty and Majestic shows:

إِنَّ ٱلْمُتَّقِينَ فِى جَنَّٰتٍ
وَعُيُونٍ ﴿١٥﴾ ءَاخِذِينَ مَآ ءَاتَىٰهُمْ رَبُّهُمْ ۚ إِنَّهُمْ كَانُوا۟ قَبْلَ ذَٰلِكَ مُحْسِنِينَ
﴿١٦﴾ كَانُوا۟ قَلِيلًا مِّنَ ٱلَّيْلِ مَا يَهْجَعُونَ ﴿١٧﴾ وَبِٱلْأَسْحَارِ هُمْ يَسْتَغْفِرُونَ
﴿١٨﴾ وَفِىٓ أَمْوَٰلِهِمْ حَقٌّ لِّلسَّآئِلِ وَٱلْمَحْرُومِ ﴿١٩﴾

[137] Note: These stories have been attributed to Ibrāhīm Ibn Adham by those that came after. So we must verify its authenticity before we rule on someone in light of these narrations otherwise any ruling on him might be an injustice.

"Indeed, the righteous will be among gardens and springs. Enjoying what their Lord has given them. Certainly, in the past they were doers of good. The part of the night they spent asleep was small. And in the hours before dawn they would pray for forgiveness. And beggers and the destitute received a due share of their wealth."

[*al-Dhāriyāt* (51): 15-19]

So He describes them as staying awake, seeking forgiveness (*istighfār*) in the early mornings, and they spend (*infāq*) from their wealth.

One of the Salaf was asleep when someone came to him and said, 'Stand up and pray! Don't you know that the keys to Paradise (*mafātīḥ al-jannah*) are with the people of the night (*ahlu'l-layl*), they are its guardians (*khuzān*), and they are its guardians.

Standing during the night brings about the high ranks (*'alu al-darajāt*) in Paradise. Allāh, the Most High said to his Prophet (ﷺ):

وَمِنَ ٱلَّيْلِ فَتَهَجَّدْ بِهِۦ
نَافِلَةً لَّكَ عَسَىٰٓ أَن يَبْعَثَكَ رَبُّكَ مَقَامًا مَّحْمُودًا ﴿٧٩﴾

"And stay awake for the prayer during part of the night, as a additional prayer for yourselft. It may well be that your Lord will raise you to a Praiseworthy Station [in the life to come]."

[*al-Isrā'* (17): 79]

So He set the reward for the night prayer (*tahajjud*) - reciting the Qur'ān in it, raising him (ﷺ) to the praiseworthy station (*maqām al-maḥmūd*), which is the highest (*a'lā*) of his (ﷺ) ranks.

'Awn Ibn 'Abdullāh said: 'Allāh will enter people into Paradise and give them until they are full. Above them will be people of higher ranks, so when they see them they will recognise them, and say: 'O our Lord they are our brethren who used be with us. So for what reason have you given them favour above us?'

So He will say: 'How far (you are from realising). Indeed, they would go hungry when you had your fill. They used to be thirsty while your thirst was quenched. They would stand at night in prayer while you would sleep. They would rise up while you were laying down.'

It (the night prayer) also makes compulsory those things of Paradise that the servant has never imagined (nor has any eye seen) in this worldly life anything similar. Allāh, the Mighty and Majestic says:

تَتَجَافَىٰ جُنُوبُهُمْ
عَنِ الْمَضَاجِعِ يَدْعُونَ رَبَّهُمْ خَوْفًا وَطَمَعًا وَمِمَّا رَزَقْنَاهُمْ
يُنفِقُونَ ﴿١٦﴾ فَلَا تَعْلَمُ نَفْسٌ مَّا أُخْفِيَ لَهُم مِّن قُرَّةِ أَعْيُنٍ جَزَاءً
بِمَا كَانُوا يَعْمَلُونَ ﴿١٧﴾

> **"Their sides draw away from [their] beds [at night], they call upon their Lord in fear and hope. And they spend on others of what We have provided for them. No soul knows what has been hidden away for them, awaiting them of comfort for eyes [i.e., satisfaction], as reward for what they used to do."**
>
> [*al-Sajdah* (32): 16-17]

In the Ṣaḥīḥ of Bukhārī it is reported from the Prophet (ﷺ)who said: "Allāh the Mighty and Majestic says: 'I have prepared for my righteous servants that which no eye has seen. Nor any ear has heard. Nor that which has occurred to the human mind.'[138] Read if you wish:

فَلَا تَعْلَمُ نَفْسٌ مَّآ أُخْفِيَ لَهُم مِّن قُرَّةِ أَعْيُنٍ جَزَآءًۢ بِمَا كَانُوا۟ يَعْمَلُونَ ﴿١٧﴾

"No soul knows what has been hidden away for them, awaiting them of comfort for eyes [i.e., satisfaction], as reward for what they used to do."
[*al-Sajdah* (32): 17]

Some of the Salaf said: 'They concealed their actions for Allāh so He concealed their reward. So when they come to it their eyes will rejoice in it.'

From the reward of those that stand at night in prayer is the abundant amount of wives from the women of Paradise (*ḥūr ul-'īn*). For the worshipper at night who leaves the pleasure of sleep and enjoyment of his wives, searching what is with Allāh, the Mighty and Majestic. So Allāh, the Most High replaces for him something better than that which he left, and that is the women of Paradise (*ḥūr ul-'īn*) in Paradise. For this reason some have said that: The length of the night prayer is like the dowry you give to them in Paradise.

Some of the Salaf would stay awake during the night and pray until they were exhausted. So someone would come to them in their sleep and say: 'O so and so, you use to stand diligently in your proposal (while praying) so what has made you fall short now?' He

[138] Bukhārī, #4780 and Muslim, #2174- 2175 on the authority of Abū Hurayrah (*raḍiyAllāhu 'anhu*).

said: 'What do you mean?' He said: 'You use to stand for prayer at night.' Did you not know that when the night worshipper stands the angels says: 'The proposer has stood to make his proposal.'

One of them saw a woman in his dream not resembling any woman in the world so he said to her: 'Who are you?' She replied: 'Hūwrā' the servant of Allāh.' So he said to her: 'Marry me.' She said: 'Propose to me and stipulate a dowry.' He said: 'And what is your dowry.' She replied: 'Lengthening the night prayer (*tul al-tahajjud*).'

One of the night worshippers (*mutahajjudūn*) fell asleep one night and saw a woman of Paradise chanting:

Do you propose to the like of me yet sleep, (stay away)
And to sleep away from those whom you love is forbidden
For we have been created for every person
That is abundant in praying and has been weakened by fasting

Another person of the Salaf would read a certain amount during the night, but once he fell asleep and saw a young girl in his sleep who had a face like the moon. She had a scroll which had something written on it. She said: 'Will you read?' He said: 'Yes.' So she gave him and he opened it and read:

Does the pleasure of sleep keep you from a better life?
With the pure women in the lofty chambers of Paradise
Living therein eternally without (fear of) death
Enjoying in gardens with fair maidens of beauty
Wake up from your dream it is better
To stand in prayer with the Qur'ān than sleeping

So he woke up and said: 'By Allāh whenever I remember her I

forgot about sleeping.'

One of the righteous would read a certain amount of the Qur'ān every night, but once he slept, so a young person stood in his dream and said in a dejected voice:

Wake up for a few hours of the night O Youth!
Perchance you will get a woman of paradise
And enjoy the bliss of an eternal place
Muḥammad and *Khalīl* (Ibrāhīm) will visit it
So stand up hour after hour
So that you can fulfil what is left of your dowry

One of the righteous Salaf who was very devout, wept for over sixty years out of longing for Allāh, so he saw himself in a dream standing on the bank of a river that was (instead of water) running with musk. Flanked by trees of pearls and plants with gold trim. All of a sudden there stood before him a group of beautiful women saying in one voice:

We were created by the God of mankind, the Lord of Muḥammad
For a people who stand during the nights
Conversing with the Lord of the worlds
Taking the worries of people while they slumber

So he said: 'Wow, wow to you all. Who are those (people)? Indeed Allāh has made you the coolness of their eyes.'

The women said: 'Don't you know them?'
He said: 'No.'

So they replied: 'Indeed these are the people that pray during the night, those of the Qur'ān and those who stay awake.'

One of the righteous would fall asleep (thereby miss a part of the night prayer) so a woman of Paradise would awaken him in his asleep and he would get up because of that.

It has been narrated about Abū Sulaymān al-Daranī that he said: 'Once my sleep took me away from my (night) prayer, before I knew it there was a woman of Paradise standing in front of me trying to wake me while saying: 'O Abū Sulaymān are you sleeping while I have been nurturing you in hiding for five hundred years?"

In another narration from him is that once he fell asleep while in prostration and he said: 'All of a sudden she was pushing me with her leg saying: 'Are you sleeping while the king is awake looking at the worshippers at night?' May the eye that prefers the pleasure of sleep over conversing with the Mighty be deprived. Stand up because the spare time is nearly over, and those that have love have met each other, so what is this sleep my beloved; coolness of my eyes. Do your eyes sleep while I nurture you in hiding since five hundred years?' He jumped up anxiously sweating from what he heard. He said: 'The sweetness of her voice is still in my hearing and heart.'[139]

Abū Sulaymān used to say: 'The people of the night have more delight (*ladha*) during the night (prayer) than the people of amusement while they amuse themselves. Had it not been for the night then I would not have wanted to remain in the world.'

Yazīd Al-Raqashī said to Ḥabīb Al-Ajmī: 'I don't know of anything more cooling to the eyes for the worshippers in the world than the night prayer, nor do I know of anything from the bliss of

[139] Note: Good dreams provide comfort and should not be understood to reflect indicators for absolute truths.

Paradise for the worshippers or more delightful to their eyes than looking at Allāh when He raises the barriers and reveals Himself.' Habib cried out and fainted.

Suri used to say: 'I have seen benefits appear during the darkness of the night.'

Abū Sulaymān said: 'When the darkness descends and all those who have love for each other are alone together, and stretch out their feet, their tears running down their cheeks, the exalted commands by calling out to Jibrīl: 'By my two eyes who are those that take delight in my words, and take comfort in conversing with me, call among them O Jibrīl-What is this weeping for?' Have you seen a person that loves to punish those that he loves? How can it befit me to punish people who when the night falls they ask of Me? So I swear that when they come forth on the Day of Judgment I will reveal my honourable face to them and they will look at me and I will look at them.'[140]

Al-Ḥasan was asked: 'Why did the people of night prayer have the most beautiful faces?'

He replied: 'That is because they are alone with the ever Merciful and He envelops them with light.'

A righteous woman saw in her dream garments that were given out to the people of the *masjid* of Muḥammad Ibn Jahadah, when the one giving them out finished he ask for a closed satchel which he opened and took out a yellow garment. She said: 'My eyes were

[140] Note: To inform about Allāh, the Mighty and Majestic is a major matter, and anything that has not been established in the authentic sources is to be disowned.

not able to see it, he made her wear it and said: This is for you because of the length of your night prayer.'

She said: 'By Allāh I use to see him (Muḥammad Ibn Jahadah) after that I would take pride in it (the garment).'

Karaz Ibn Wabrah said: 'It has reached me that Ka'b said: 'Indeed the angels gaze from the sky to those praying the night prayer, as you gaze at the stars at night.'

O soul the righteous have succeeded with piety
They see the truth while my heart is blind
O their beauty all the while the night covers them
Their light outshining the stars
They chant with remembrance at night
So their life is made pleasant with that reciting
Their hearts dedicated to remembrance (of Allāh)
Their tears like a constant stream of pearls
Like the rising of dawn when it breaks
And to take from it forgiveness is the best fate

In some narrations Allāh, the Mighty and Majestic says every night: 'O Jibrīl wake up so and so and put to sleep so and so.'

One of the righteous stood up during a cold night while wearing shabby garments and was struck by cold so he began to weep. He heard a voice call out to him saying: 'We woke you up and put others to sleep, yet you cry?'

Wake up you! deserving of my love
How many are sleep then wake up to the dew of Najd
How far between are the one's alone and the one that's stays awake
And the one in slumber; the hiding and the beginner

It was said to Ibn Mas'ūd (*raḍiyAllāhu 'anhu*): 'We are unable to stand in the night prayer.'

To which he replied: 'Your sins have taken you far away.'

It was also said to Al-Ḥasan: 'We are unable to stand at night to pray.'

He said: 'Your sins have tied you down. Indeed the kings are only in the privacy (*khalwa*) of those that who are sincere in their love and interaction. As for the one who opposes them then they are not pleased with them.'

The night is for me and for those that I love so that
I may converse with them
I have chosen them so they may hear me and understand me
They have hearts full of secrets
They impress on my love and advice
The trees of understanding bear fruit for them
They achieve not what they achieve except they raise themselves
They are pleased, not weakened or incapable
And keep hold of the rope to get near me and don't stop

CHAPTER SIX

[Mention of the Supplications made in the Ḥadīth]

It is:

«اللهم إني أسألُكَ فعلَ الخيرات، وترك المنكرات، وحُبَّ المساكين، وأَنْ تَغْفِرَ لي وتَرْحَمَني، وإذا أردت فتنةً في قومٍ فتوفَّني غيرَ مفتون، وأسألك حُبَّك وحُبَّ من يُحِبُّكَ وحُبَّ عملٍ يقرِّبني إلى حبِّكَ»

> "O Allāh I ask you (the ability to) do good actions, leaving bad actions, (having) love of the needy, that you forgive me and have mercy upon me. When you wish a calamity to befall a people to take my life without being put to trial. I ask you for your love and the love of the one who loves you and love of those actions that will draw me closer to your love."

The Prophet (ﷺ) said: "Indeed it is the truth, so study it and learn it."

This is a great supplication (*du'ā' 'aẓīm*) from the most comprehensive and complete of supplications (*ajmah' al-'adiyah wa akmal*).

In his statement:

اللهم إني أسألك فعل الخيرات، وترك المنكرات،

"I ask you (the ability for doing) good actions and leaving bad actions."

This supplication *(du'ā')* contains all types good (*khayr*) and the leaving off of all types of evil (*sharr*). For good deeds include all that which Allāh, the Most High loves. And what draws a person near to Him in the form of actions *(a'māl)* and statements *(aqwāl)* that are obligatory *(wājibāt)* or recommended *(mustahabāt)*. While evil deeds *(munkarāt)* includes all that which Allāh, the Most High hates. Such actions and statements that lead a person far away from Allāh. So whoever attains the request as this supplication has indeed attained goodness of this life and the next.

The Prophet (ﷺ) used to like such concise supplications. As 'Ā'ishah *(raḍiyAllāhu 'anhā)* said: 'The Prophet (ﷺ) use to like the concise supplications and leave what which was not.' Reported by Abū Dāwūd.[141] The statement:

وحُبَّ المساكين،

"Love of the needy"

It can be said that this already comes under the general term of good deeds *(fi'l al-khayrāt)*. It has been singled out in mention here in order to show its importance *(quwa)* and value *(sharf)*. As the love of Allāh, the Most High, is mentioned along with what He loves *(ḥubb)* and actions that will help a person attain His love. This is the true essence *(aṣl)* of all good deeds *(fi'l al-khayrāt)*. It has also been said that it is a request from Allāh, the Mighty and Majestic to provide him with the actions of obedience *(a'māl al-ṭā'āt)* with the limbs *(jawāriḥ)* and leaving off bad deeds *(tark al-munkarāt)*

[141] Abū Dāwūd, #1482.

of the limbs, and also that which leads to it. All of which is His love, the love of what He loves and actions that lead to His love. This love in the heart (*qalb*) brings about the undertaking of good actions by the limbs and the avoidance of bad actions. He also asked Allāh, the Most High to make him love the actions which will attain His love.

This supplication (*du'ā'*) contains the request (*sawāl*) of Allāh's love (*ḥubb*), the love of those whom He loves, the love of those actions which draw a person near to His love and love of it. All of which is made necessary by doing good deeds.

Whereas leaving off bad deeds implies safety (*salāma*) from tribulations (*fitan*); which in turn implies avoiding all evil. So (this) gathers together seeking (*ṭalab*) all good of this life.

It also including the seeking of forgiveness (*maghfira*) and mercy (*raḥma*) which is all the best of the Hereafter. Thereby containing an invocation for the best of this life and the next.

The intent behind *'loving the needy'* is in essence love (*aṣl al-ḥubb*) of Allāh, the Most High, because the needy and poor have nothing which can cause others to love them for His sake. So they do not love except for Allāh's sake. And love for Allāh is the strongest bonds of faith (*awthaq 'arā al-īmān*). It is also from among the signs of tasting (*dhawq*) the sweetness of faith (*ḥalawa al-īmān*), which is true faith (*sarīḥ al-īmān*). It is the best type of faith [142] (*afḍal al-īmān*), all of which is reported from the Prophet (ﷺ) and that he described it as loving for the sake of Allāh, the Most High.

[142] From that is the narration: "The strongest bond of faith is love for Allāh's sake." Aḥmad in his *Musnad*, 4/286 on the authority of Barā' Ibn 'Aazib (*raḍiyAllāhu 'anhu*). Reported by Aḥmad, 5/247 and others on the authority of Mu'ādh (*raḍiyAllāhu 'anhu*). Reported by Aḥmad, 5/146 and Abū Dāwūd, #4599

It was narrated on the authority of Ibn ʿAbbās (*raḍiyAllāhu ʿanhumā*) who said: 'With it (love) you will attain the guardianship (*wilāya*) of Allāh, and with it you find the sweetness of faith (*taʿm al-īmān*).'[143]

Love of the needy is something the Prophet (ﷺ) advised his Companions. Abū Dharr (*raḍiyAllāhu ʿanhu*) said: 'The Messenger of Allāh (ﷺ) advised me to love the poor, the needy and to get close to them. Reported by Imām Aḥmad.[144]

Reported by Tirmidhī[145] on the authority of ʿĀ'ishah (*raḍiyAllāhu ʿanhā*) that the Prophet (ﷺ) said to her: "O ʿĀ'ishah love the needy and get close to them for indeed Allāh will draw you close on the Day of Judgment."

It has also been narrated that [Prophet] Dāwūd (*ʿalayhis-salām*) use to sit with the poor people and say: 'O Lord, a poor person (referring to himself) amongst the poor.'

---

on the authority of Abū Dharr (*raḍiyAllāhu ʿanhu*). Reported by Ṭayalisī, #378, and Ṭabarānī in *Al-Kabīr*, 10/10357, 10531, and in *Al-Ṣagīr*, 1/223-224. Also in Ḥākim, 2/380 on the authority of Ibn Masʿūd (*raḍiyAllāhu ʿanhu).*

Ḥākim said: This ḥadīth has an authentic chain even though Bukhārī and Muslim did not report it in their books. Al-Dhahabī added to this: This is not authentic. Saʿaq, although reliable, his teacher is rejected in ḥadīth. So said Bukhārī. Haythamī said in *Majmaʿ*, 1/90, 163: In the chain is ʿAqīl Ibn Al-Jaʿad about whom Bukhārī said: His narrations are rejected.

Haythamī said, 7/260-261: Ṭabarānī narrated it with two chains. One of the chains has reliable narrators other than Bakīr Ibn Maʿrūf, he is considered reliable by Aḥmad and others, although he has weakness.

[143] Reported by Ibn Al-Mubarak in *al-Zuhd*, #353.

[144] Aḥmad in his *Musnad*, 5/159. Haythamī said, 10/263: Narrated by Aḥmad and Ṭabarānī in *Al-Awsaṭ*, and one of the chains of narrations of Aḥmad's has reliable narrators.

[145] Tirmidhī, #2352 and he said: This narration is strange (garīb). Al-Ḥāfiẓ said In *Talkhīs*, 3/109: The chain of narration is weak.

The righteous Salaf never ceased counselling others to love the poor. Sufyān Al-Thawrī wrote to some of his brothers: 'You should take care of the poor, the needy and stay close to them because the Messenger of Allāh (ﷺ) used to ask His Lord for the love of the needy.'

Loving the poor brings about sincerity of actions (*ikhlāṣ al-aʿmāl*) for Allāh, the Most High. Sincerity (*ikhlāṣ*) is the very basis of actions (*asās al-aʿmāl*) without it actions are not accepted. Indeed love of those in need ensures that it provides them with benefit of whatever is possible from the benefits of this world and the next. So when they attain (characteristic of) giving benefit (*nafʿ*) to others, loving them and being kind (*iḥsān*) towards them then this action brings out sincerity (*khāliṣ*). The Qur'ān shows this as Allāh, the Mighty and Majestic says:

وَيُطْعِمُونَ ٱلطَّعَامَ عَلَىٰ حُبِّهِۦ مِسْكِينًا
وَيَتِيمًا وَأَسِيرًا ﴿٨﴾ إِنَّمَا نُطْعِمُكُمْ لِوَجْهِ ٱللَّهِ لَا نُرِيدُ مِنكُمْ جَزَآءً وَلَا شُكُورًا

"They give food, despite their love for it to the poor, and the orphans and the prisoner. [Saying], 'We feed you only out of desire for the countenance [i.e., approval] of Allāh alone. We do not want any repayment from you, nor any thanks."

[*al-Insān* (76): 8-9]

And He says:

وَلَا تَطْرُدِ ٱلَّذِينَ يَدْعُونَ رَبَّهُم بِٱلْغَدَوٰةِ وَٱلْعَشِىِّ يُرِيدُونَ
وَجْهَهُۥ ۖ مَا عَلَيْكَ مِنْ حِسَابِهِم مِّن شَىْءٍ وَمَا مِنْ حِسَابِكَ
عَلَيْهِم مِّن شَىْءٍ فَتَطْرُدَهُمْ فَتَكُونَ مِنَ ٱلظَّٰلِمِينَ ﴿٥٢﴾

"And do not chase away those who call upon their Lord morning and afternoon, seeking His Face.

Their reckoning is in no way your responsibility and your reckoning is in no way their responsibility. So if you did chase them away, you would be among the wrong-doers [unjust].”

[*al-An'ām* (6): 52]

And the Most High says:

وَٱصْبِرْ نَفْسَكَ مَعَ ٱلَّذِينَ يَدْعُونَ رَبَّهُم بِٱلْغَدَوٰةِ وَٱلْعَشِىِّ يُرِيدُونَ وَجْهَهُۥ ۖ وَلَا تَعْدُ عَيْنَاكَ عَنْهُمْ تُرِيدُ زِينَةَ ٱلْحَيَوٰةِ ٱلدُّنْيَا ۖ

“Restrain yourself patiently [by being] with those who call upon their Lord in the morning and evening, desiring His Face. And do not let your eyes overlook them, desiring the pomp and glitter of this worldly life.”

[*al-Kahf* (18): 28]

Sa'd Ibn Abī Waqqāṣ (*raḍiyAllāhu 'anhu*) said: 'This verse was revealed regarding six people. Regarding me; ['Abdullah] Ibn Mas'ūd; Suhayb [al-Rumī]; 'Ammār [Ibn Yāsir]; Miqdād [Ibn Aswad] and Bilāl [Ibn Rabah] (*raḍiyAllāhu 'anhu*).' The Quraysh said to the Messenger of Allāh (ﷺ): 'We are not happy to be followers of you along with them, so turn them away from you.' So Allāh revealed:

وَلَا تَطْرُدِ ٱلَّذِينَ يَدْعُونَ رَبَّهُم بِٱلْغَدَوٰةِ وَٱلْعَشِىِّ يُرِيدُونَ وَجْهَهُۥ ۖ

“And do not chase away those who call upon their Lord morning and afternoon, seeking His Face.”

[*al-An'ām* (6): 52]

Khabāb Ibn Al-Arat (*raḍiyAllāhu 'anhu*) said concerning this verse:

'Al-Aqra' Ibn Ḥābis and 'Uyanah Ibn Ḥisn arrived and found the Messenger of Allāh (ﷺ) sitting among the weak (and poor) believers such as Suhayb, 'Ammār, Bilāl and Khabāb. When they saw who was with the Prophet (ﷺ) they belittled them. So they came to him (the Prophet) and when they were alone with him.' They then said: 'We would like you to arrange for us a sitting that the Arabs would recognise our status. These (other) people from the (low class of) Arabs come to you, we are ashamed to be seen by the Arabs with these slaves. So when we come to you make them depart away from you. When we finish our sittings with you, then you may go back and sit with them, if you wish.' He (ﷺ) said: 'Yes.' Then they said: 'Write it down for us.' So he called for something to be written it down, and while we were sitting in a corner Jibrīl (*'alayhis-salām*) came down with the verse and said:

وَلَا تَطْرُدِ ٱلَّذِينَ يَدْعُونَ رَبَّهُم بِٱلْغَدَوٰةِ وَٱلْعَشِيِّ يُرِيدُونَ
وَجْهَهُۥ ۖ مَا عَلَيْكَ مِنْ حِسَابِهِم مِّن شَىْءٍ وَمَا مِنْ حِسَابِكَ
عَلَيْهِم مِّن شَىْءٍ فَتَطْرُدَهُمْ فَتَكُونَ مِنَ ٱلظَّٰلِمِينَ ﴿٥٢﴾

"And do not chase away those who call upon their Lord morning and afternoon, seeking His Face. Their reckoning is in no way your responsibility and your reckoning is in no way their responsibility. So if you did chase them away, you would be among the wrong-doers [unjust]"

[*al-An'ām* (6): 52]

Then Jibrīl mentioned Al-Aqra' Ibn Ḥābis and 'Uyanah Ibn Ḥisn said:

وَكَذَٰلِكَ فَتَنَّا بَعْضَهُم بِبَعْضٍ لِّيَقُولُوٓا۟ أَهَٰٓؤُلَآءِ مَنَّ ٱللَّهُ
عَلَيْهِم مِّنۢ بَيْنِنَآ ۗ أَلَيْسَ ٱللَّهُ بِأَعْلَمَ بِٱلشَّٰكِرِينَ ﴿٥٣﴾

"In this way We try some of them by means of others, so that they might say, 'Are these the people among us to whom Allāh has bestowed His favour upon?' Does not Allāh know best as to who is thankful [to Him]?"

[*al-An'ām* (6): 53]

He also said:

وَإِذَا جَآءَكَ ٱلَّذِينَ يُؤْمِنُونَ بِـَٔايَـٰتِنَا فَقُلْ سَلَـٰمٌ عَلَيْكُمْ ۖ كَتَبَ رَبُّكُمْ عَلَىٰ نَفْسِهِ ٱلرَّحْمَةَ ۖ

"And when those who believe in Our Signs come to you, say, 'Peace be upon you!' Your Lord has decreed mercy incumbent upon Himself."

[*al-An'ām* (6): 54]

He [Khabāb] said: 'We came close to him until we put our knees next to his knees. The Messenger (ﷺ) used to sit with us and when he wished to leave he would get up and leave us, so Allāh revealed the verse:

وَٱصْبِرْ نَفْسَكَ مَعَ ٱلَّذِينَ يَدْعُونَ رَبَّهُم بِٱلْغَدَوٰةِ وَٱلْعَشِىِّ يُرِيدُونَ وَجْهَهُۥ ۖ وَلَا تَعْدُ عَيْنَاكَ عَنْهُمْ

"Restrain yourself patiently [by being] with those who call upon their Lord in the morning and evening, desiring His Face. And do not let your eyes overlook them, desiring the pomp and glitter of this worldly life."

[*al-Kahf* (18): 28]

Sitting with the noble people:

وَلَا تُطِعْ مَنْ أَغْفَلْنَا قَلْبَهُۥ عَن ذِكْرِنَا وَٱتَّبَعَ هَوَىٰهُ وَكَانَ أَمْرُهُۥ فُرُطًا ﴿٢٨﴾

"And do not obey someone whose heart We have made neglectful of Our remembrance and who follows his own whims and desire and whose life has transgressed all bounds."

[*al-Kahf* (18): 28]

Meaning 'Uyanah and Al-Aqra'.

Khabāb (*raḍiyAllāhu 'anhu*) said: 'We use to sit with the Prophet (ﷺ) and after an hour or so we would stand and leave, and so would we.' Reported by Ibn Mājah[146] and others.[147]

The Prophet (ﷺ) use to visit the sick from among the needy of the people of Madīnah and follow their funeral processions. He would never decline walking with widows and the needy until their needs were fulfilled.[148] It was upon this guidance the Companions (*raḍiyAllāhu 'anhu*) and those after them followed.

146 Ibn Mājah, #4127.

147 Ibn Abī Ḥātim in his explanation, as is in the explanation of Ibn Kathīr, 2/134-135, and Ibn Jarīr in his explanation, 7/127-128. Ibn Kathīr said in his explanation, 2/135: this is a strange ḥadīth, this verse is from the Makkan period and Al-Aqra' Ibn Ḥābis and 'Uyanah accepted Islām after the migration by some time.

148 Dārimī, 1/35, Nasā'ī, 3/109, and Ḥākim, 2/614 on the authority of 'Abdullāh Ibn Abī Awfah (*raḍiyAllāhu 'anhu*) and said: 'Authentic to the level of Bukhārī and Muslim, but they did not include it in their books (the Ṣaḥīḥ of Bukhārī and Muslim).'

It has been narrated on the authority of Abū Hurayrah (*raḍiyAllāhu ʿanhu*) who said: "Jaʿfar Ibn Abī Ṭālib use to love the needy and sitting with them, talking with them, and the Prophet (ﷺ) use to nickname him Abū Masakīn (father of the needy)." [152]

In another narration: "He used to feed them, sometimes take out to them *ʿakkah*[150] of honey they would open it up and eat it clean."[151]

Zainab Bint Khuzaymah (*raḍiyAllāhu ʿanhā*) the mother of the believers was called the mother of the needy due to the abundant amount of kindness (*iḥsān*) she showed them, and she died during the lifetime of the Prophet (ﷺ).

Ḍharar Ibn Murrah said in his description of ʿAlī Ibn Abī Ṭālib during the days of his caliphate: 'He used to hold in high esteem the people of religion and love the poor.'

His son Al-Ḥasan [Ibn ʿAlī] (*raḍiyAllāhu ʿanhumā*) walked past the needy eating and they invited him to join them so he did. He then read the verse:

إِنَّهُۥ لَا يُحِبُّ ٱلْمُسْتَكْبِرِينَ ﴿٢٣﴾

"Indeed, He does not like the arrogant."

---

[149] Tirmidhī, #3766 and said: 'This ḥadīth is strange.' Abū Isḥāq Al-Makhzūmi who is Ibrāhīm Ibn Fuḍayl Al-Madanī

[150] Round container made from leather used for carrying fat and honey.

[151] Something similar was reported by Bukhārī, #5432 on the authority of Abū Hurayrah (*raḍiyAllāhu ʿanhu*).

Then he invited them to his house, fed them and was very generous towards them.

Ibn 'Umar (*raḍiyAllāhu 'anhumā*) used to only eat with poor people, and he use to say: 'Maybe one of these people will be a king on the Day of Judgment.'

A poor blind person came to Ibn Mas'ūd (*raḍiyAllāhu 'anhu*), at a time when there was already a crowd around him, and he called him: 'O Abū 'Abdu'l-Raḥmān! It seems you have befriended people of fine clothes while you have dismissed me because I am a pauper. So he said 'Come close'. He kept coming close until he sat him right next him.'

Mutrif Ibn 'Abdullāh use to wear fine clothes then go and sit with the poor people.

Sufyān Al-Thawrī use to honour poor people and avoid people of this worldly life. So the poor were like rich people in his gatherings and the rich were like they were poor.

Sulaymān Al-Taymī said: 'When we searched for our companions we found them with the poor and needy.'

Fuḍayl said: 'Whoever wishes for honour in the Hereafter then let him sit with the needy.'

From the virtues of the needy is that they are the majority of the people of Paradise (*ahlu'l-jannah*) as the Prophet (ﷺ) said: "I stood by a door of paradise and found that most of those that entered were poor."[152]

He (ﷺ) also said: "Paradise and Hell fire argued. Paradise said: 'Only the weak and poor enter me.'"[153]

The Prophet (ﷺ) was asked about the people of Paradise so he said: "Every weak humble person."[154]

They are the first people that will enter Paradise as is authentically reported from the Prophet (ﷺ): "The poor people will enter Paradise before the rich by forty years."[155]

In another narration: "They will enter Paradise by half a day, which is five-hundred years."[156]

They will be the first people to arrive at the pool (*al-ḥawd*), as the Prophet (ﷺ) said: "The first people to come to the pool are:

---

[152] Part of a ḥadīth reported by Bukhārī, #6547 and Muslim, #2736 from the narration of Usamah Ibn Zayd (*raḍiyAllāhu 'anhu*).

[153] Muslim, #4918/34

[154] Bukhārī, #4918 and Muslim, #2853 from the ḥadīth of Ḥārithah Ibn Wahb Al-Khaza'ī (*raḍiyAllāhu 'anhu*).

[155] Muslim, #2979 from the ḥadīth of 'Abdullāh Ibn 'Amr (*raḍiyAllāhu 'anhumā*) with the wording: 'The poor of the Muhājirūn will enter Paradise before the rich people by forty years.'

[156] Aḥmad, 2/343-451, and Tirmidhī, #2353, #2354 and he said: 'This ḥadīth is authentic.' In another narration: Authentic and Nasā'ī in *Al-Kubrah* as in *Tuḥfahtu-Ashrāf*, 11/6 and Ibn Mājah, #4122 from the ḥadīth of Abū Hurayrah (*raḍiyAllāhu 'anhu*).

The poor *Muhājirūn* (those with dirty clothes and hair unkempt)[157] those who the luxurious women do not marry, nor do doors open for them."[158]

They are the followers of the Messengers as Allāh, Most High informs us in the Qur'ān about Nūḥ (*'alayhis-salām*) that his nation taunted him because of the weak people that followed him:

قَالُوٓا۟ أَنُؤْمِنُ لَكَ وَٱتَّبَعَكَ ٱلْأَرْذَلُونَ ﴿١١١﴾

"They said: 'Should we believe you while you are followed by the lowest [class of people]?'"

[*al-Shu'arā'* (26): 111]

Likewise when Heraclius questioned Abū Sufyān about the Prophet (ﷺ) whether noble people followed him or the weak. So he replied: 'The weak.' So Hercules said: 'They are the followers of the Messengers.'[159]

They are better than the people of wealth in the opinion of many if not most of the scholars. Many evidences point towards that conclusion. From them is the statement of the Prophet (ﷺ) while

---

157 Found In *Usūl*: (Their heads are soiled and the hair dishevelled.) which is wrong. What is verified is from the sources of references.

158 Aḥmad in his *Musnad*, 5/275-276, and Tirmidhī, #2444, and he said: This ḥadīth is strange from this angle. This ḥadīth is also been narrated by Mi'dan Ibn Abī Ṭalḥah on the authority of Thawbān (*raḍiyAllāhu 'anhu*) from the Prophet (ﷺ). Also Abū Salam Al-Habashī whose name was Mamtūr from the area of Shām. Also in Ibn Mājah, #4304, and Ḥākim, 4/184 he said: 'This ḥadīth has an authentic chain although not in Bukhārī or Muslim from the ḥadīth of Abū Salām Mamtūr from Thawbān (*raḍiyAllāhu 'anhu*).

159 Bukhārī, #7 and Muslim, #1773 from the ḥadīth of Ibn 'Abbās (*raḍiyAllāhu 'anhumā*) on the authority of Abū Sufyān (*raḍiyAllāhu 'anhu*).

he was passing by a poor person and a rich person in the *masjid*: "This (poor person) is better than the earth full of that type of person (i.e. the rich person)." Reported by Bukhārī[160] and others.[161]

Also if (a needy person) was to take an oath invoking Allāh then Allāh would fulfil it for him as (shown) in the ḥadīth of Bukhārī from the Prophet (ﷺ) who said about the people of Paradise: "Every weak and humble person that if he would take an oath upon Allāh it would be fulfilled by Allāh."[162]

In another narration: "Dishevelled hair and shabby clothes."[163] And in another narration reported by Ibn Mājah: "They are the kings of Paradise (*muluk al-jannah*)."[164]

And In the famous ḥadīth: "Perhaps are person with unkempt hair, dusty and wearing shabby clothes that is pushed away from (people's) doors were to take an oath upon Allāh, that Allāh would

---

[160] Bukhārī, #6447 on the authority of Sahl Ibn Sa'd (*raḍiyAllāhu 'anhu*).

[161] Ibn Mājah, #4120.

[162] The reference for this has already preceded.

[163] Aḥmad in his *Musnad*, 3/145 from the ḥadīth of Anas (*raḍiyAllāhu 'anhu*). Haythamī said, 10/264: In the chain is Ibn Luhay'ah and his narrations are supported. Ibn Mājah reported it in, #4110 and Ṭabarānī in *Al-Kabīr*, 20/84, from the ḥadīth of Mu'ādh Ibn Jabal (*raḍiyAllāhu 'anhu*) from the Prophet (ﷺ): "Should I not inform you of the kings of Paradise?" I said: 'Of course.' So he said: "A weak and humble man with shabby clothes." Al-'Irāqī said in his checking of *Al-Iḥyā'*, 4/198: The chain is good. Also refer to narrations that mention shabby clothes in *Al-Majma'*, 10/264-265.

[164] Ibn Mājah, #4110.

fulfil it." Reported by Ḥākim[165] and others.[166]

Maybe a man wearing shabby clothes that are worn out,

Saves the world from his evil
He is seen as a rich person
Even though he owns naught
And if he was to take an oath for something
Then Allāh would fulfil it for him

Ibn Mas'ūd (*raḍiyAllāhu 'anhu*) said: 'Be people of refreshed hearts, simple clothes, praying at night, with lamps in the darkness, known by the inhabitants of the heavens and unknown by the those on earth.'

Glad tidings for the servants that holds firm onto the rope of Allāh
His feet firmly planted along the straight path
Worn out clothes and a new heart hidden
On earth but well known to the inhabitants of the heavens
Dismissing the life of this world with ardour
Until he raises up to the next life with all zeal
That person is greater than the one wearing a crown reclining
On cushions being entertained by his servants

---

165 Ḥākim, 4/328 and he said: 'This ḥadīth has an authentic chain, and I think Muslim reported it from the ḥadīth of Ḥafs Ibn 'Abdullāh Ibn Anas.'

166 Abū Nu'aym in *al-Ḥilyah*, 1/7 from the ḥadīth of Abū Hurayrah (*raḍiyAllāhu 'anhu*) with the wording: and the eyes of the people find repugnant. Reported by Ṭabarānī in *Al-Awsaṭ*, #861 and he said: 'No one but Usāmah narrated this ḥadīth from Ḥafs.' Haythamī said in *Al-Majma'*, 10/264: In the chain is 'Abdullāh Ibn Mūsā Al-Taymī and he is regarded as reliable. The rest of the narrators are narrators of Bukhārī with the exception of Jariyah Ibn Ḥarām, who was regarded as reliable by Ibn Ḥibbān in spite of his weakness.

Reported by Al-Bazzār in *Bahr Al-Zukhar*, #2035 from the ḥadīth of Ibn Mas'ūd (*raḍiyAllāhu 'anhu*) and he said: These words we have only come to know of through 'Abdullāh with this chain of narration.

Know that loving the poor has many benefits among which are: It makes a person sincere (*ikhlāṣ*) in his actions for Allāh, the Mighty and Majestic. Being kind to them out of love for them is only for Allāh, the Mighty and Majestic. Quite often, no one seeks reward from the poor in this life. As for the one who shows them kindness in order to be praised, then he does so not out of love for them, rather it is out of love for the people of this world and seeking their praise by loving the needy.

Also [from the benefits of loving the poor] is that it removes arrogance (*kibr*). For indeed the arrogant person is not happy to sit with the poor as preceded with the heads of Quraysh, the Bedouins and those that follow them from this nation and imitate them. Even some of the evil scholars would not attend the congregation prayers out of fear that poor people would stand next to them in the line for the prayer.

This arrogance would prevent them from many other good actions. Such as attending the gatherings of knowledge and remembrance which would be frequented by poor people. So the arrogant one would miss these gatherings due to his arrogance. Maybe the case would be, that most of the poor people would hear from him knowledge (*'ilm*) and remembrance (*dhikr*). While the people of arrogance turn up their noses at these gatherings thereby missing much good.

Allāh, the Most High has informed us about what the idolaters said:

وَقَالُوا۟
لَوْلَا نُزِّلَ هَٰذَا ٱلْقُرْءَانُ عَلَىٰ رَجُلٍ مِّنَ ٱلْقَرْيَتَيْنِ عَظِيمٍ ﴿٣١﴾

"And they said: 'Why was this Qur'ān not sent

down upon a great man from [one of] the two cities?"'

[*al-Zukhruf* (43): 31]

They were hinting at the great men of Makkah and Taif such as: 'Utbah Ibn Rabī'ah and his brother Shaybah and the like, from the brave men of Quraysh and Thaqīf who had wealth and status more than Muḥammad (ﷺ) and a greater claim to leadership. Allāh rejects this by saying that they are trying to share out the mercy of Allāh as they themselves saw fit. He also informs them that He raises the ranks of some over others in this life and likewise in the hereafter. And that His mercy of Prophethood (*nabuwa*); knowledge (*'ilm*) and faith (*īmān*) is better than what they gather from the wealth of this world which will eventually perish. Allāh chooses who to bestow His religious mercy (*raḥma*) from the people of the world. He chose Muḥammad (ﷺ) and did not choose anyone else to share with him those favours. As He says:

وَأَنزَلَ ٱللَّهُ عَلَيْكَ ٱلْكِتَٰبَ وَٱلْحِكْمَةَ وَعَلَّمَكَ
مَا لَمْ تَكُن تَعْلَمُ ۚ وَكَانَ فَضْلُ ٱللَّهِ عَلَيْكَ عَظِيمًا ﴿١١٣﴾

"Allāh has revealed to you the Book and wisdom and has taught you what you did not know before. And Allāh's favour upon you is indeed immense."

[*al-Nisā'* (4): 113]

'Alī Ibn Al-Ḥusayn use to sit in the gathering of Zayd Ibn Aslam and was rebuked for doing so, so he said: 'A person should sit wherever there is benefit (hinting that he benefitted from listening to knowledge and wisdom that he did not previously hear)'. Zayd Ibn Aslam's father was the freed slave of 'Umar and 'Alī Ibn Al-Ḥusayn was a leader of the tribe of Hashim and their noble.

When Al-Zuhrī and Abū Hāzim the ascetic came together in Madīnah with some of the tribesmen of Banu Umayyah (during *ḥajj*) Zuhrī heard the words of Abū Hāzim and his wisdom, he was impressed by him. So he stated: 'He has been my neighbour for such and such a time yet I have not sat with him or knew he had this knowledge.' Abū Hāzim said to him: 'I am from the poor people, had I been from the rich or wealthy you would have heard of me!' he rebuked him for it (not knowing about him).'

In a narration from him he said: 'If you loved Allāh, you would have loved me. However you forgot Allāh and you forgot me.' Indicating by this that whoever loves Allāh, the Most High, loves the poor and needy from the people of knowledge (*ahlul-'ilm*) and wisdom (*ḥikmah*) due to their love of Allāh, the Most High. Whosoever is heedless (*ghāfil*) of Allāh and His close allies from the poor people, does not raise an eyebrow for them, will not benefit from the beneficial knowledge (*al-'ulum al-nāfi'*) and wisdom that Allāh has bestowed on them, and it is not to be found with anyone else in the world.

The scholars from among the Salaf used to take knowledge from its people, most of them were poor and did not possess any wealth or status in this world. They would avoid the people of authority and power, and did not take anything from their knowledge at all.

Also from [the benefits of loving the poor] are: It brings about the rectification the heart (*ṣilāḥ al-qalb*) and devotion (*khushu'*). In the *Musnad* it is reported on the authority of Abū Hurayrah (*raḍiyAllāhu 'anhu*) that a man complained to the Messenger of Allāh (ﷺ) about the hardness (*qaṣwa*) of his heart. So he said to him: "If you wish your heart to be softer then feed the poor and rub the head of an orphan."[167]

Also from [the benefits of loving the poor] are: Sitting with the poor makes the person sitting with them pleased with the provisions that Allāh, the Mighty and Majestic has given them. Also the favours (*ni'ma*) of Allāh he has are magnified in his eyes because he sees those lower than him in the world. While sitting with rich people makes a person angry with what Allāh has given him. He extends his eyes to look at the beauty of what they have and what they enjoy. Whereas Allāh, the Mighty and Majestic has forbade his Prophet (ﷺ) from that:

وَلَا تَمُدَّنَّ عَيْنَيْكَ إِلَىٰ مَا مَتَّعْنَا بِهِۦٓ أَزْوَٰجًا مِّنْهُمْ زَهْرَةَ ٱلْحَيَوٰةِ ٱلدُّنْيَا لِنَفْتِنَهُمْ فِيهِ ۚ وَرِزْقُ رَبِّكَ خَيْرٌ وَأَبْقَىٰ ﴿١٣١﴾

"Do not extend your eyes longingly toward that which We have given certain of them to enjoy, the splendour of worldly life in order that We may test them by it. Your Lord's provision is better and longer lasting."

[*Ṭāhā* (20): 131]

And the Prophet (ﷺ) said: "Look at those who are below you (who have less than you) and do not look at those who are above you (those who have more than you), because it is less likely that you will look down on the favours of Allāh upon you."[168]

[167] Aḥmad in his *Musnad*, 2/263, 387 by way of Abū 'Imrān Al-Jawnī from Rijl on the authority of Abū Hurayrah (*raḍiyAllāhu 'anhu*). In another narration also in *Musnad* of Aḥmad: From Abū 'Imrān on the authority of Abū Hurayrah (*raḍiyAllāhu 'anhu*) without mentioning the second person in the chain. Haythamī said in *Al-Majma'*, 8/160: It narrators are used by Bukhārī.

Abū Dharr (*raḍiyAllāhu 'anhu*) said: 'The Messenger of Allāh (ﷺ) advised me to look at those who were lesser-off than me and not at those who were better-off than me. He also advised me to love the poor and stay close to them.'[169]

'Awn Ibn 'Abdullāh Ibn 'Utbah Ibn Mas'ūd used to sit with wealthy people and was always sad. This is because he would always look at those who had better clothes than him, better riding beast than him, better place to live and better food to eat. So he left their gatherings and began to sit with the poor, were he found happiness .

It is also narrated from the Prophet (ﷺ) that he forbade 'Ā'ishah (*raḍiyAllāhu 'anhā*) from mixing with rich people.[170]

'Umar (*raḍiyAllāhu 'anhu*) said: 'Beware of entering upon (mixing with) people of wealth, for indeed it makes one ungrateful with his provisions.'

Know that the word poor person (*miskīn*) in general means someone who does not have enough wealth to suffice their basic

[168] Muslim, 9/2963 from the ḥadīth of Abū Hurayrah (*raḍiyAllāhu 'anhu*).

[169] The reference has preceded.

[170] Tirmidhī, #1780 and Ḥākim, 4/312, and Ibn Al-Jawzī in *Mawdhu'āt*, 3/139-140 on the authority of 'Ā'ishah (*raḍiyAllāhu 'anhā*) who said: 'The Prophet (ﷺ) said to me: "If you want to join me then suffice with provisions as much as one riding beast can carry, and beware of siting with wealthy people."'

Tirmidhī said: This ḥadīth is strange and we do not know if it except from Ṣaliḥ Ibn Ḥasan. He said: I heard Muḥammad (al-Bukhārī) say: Ṣaliḥ Ibn Ḥasan is not accepted as a narrator of ḥadīth. Ḥākim said: This chain of narration is authentic but not included in Bukhārī and Muslim. Al-Dhahabī added to this by saying: Sa'īd Ibn Muḥammad does not exist.

needs for himself. The need makes him deprived (*maḥrūm*) and humble (*tawāḍiʿ*), as opposed to the wealth of the rich person it leads him to tyranny. This is why the poor person is blameworthy [sinful] for being arrogant and the threat of punishment is far greater because he has gone against what his poverty negates which is self-conceitedness (*ikhtiyāl*), boasting (*zahw*) and pride (*kibr*).

In view of the fact that the word *'miskīn'* only applies in general terms to the person who does not have enough to suffice (his needs). Allāh, the Most High has recommended that one should give them preference and feed them. He has praised those that feed them, and rebuked those who do not feed them. He also made a portion for them in charity (*ṣadaqah*), war booty (*fa'i*). a fifth (*khums*) of the war booty (*ghanā'im*) [which is taken for the Messenger] and when someone's will is divided that they keep the poor in mind and try to help them. The poor fall into two categories:

The first type: The one who is in need but it is not apparent until he makes it known to people.

The second type: The one who conceals his need and gives the impression he is not in need of anything. This is the more honourable of the two types. Allāh has praised such a person in His statement:

لِلْفُقَرَآءِ ٱلَّذِينَ أُحْصِرُوا۟ فِى سَبِيلِ ٱللَّهِ
لَا يَسْتَطِيعُونَ ضَرْبًا فِى ٱلْأَرْضِ يَحْسَبُهُمُ
ٱلْجَاهِلُ أَغْنِيَآءَ مِنَ ٱلتَّعَفُّفِ تَعْرِفُهُم بِسِيمَٰهُمْ
لَا يَسْـَٔلُونَ ٱلنَّاسَ إِلْحَافًا ۗ وَمَا تُنفِقُوا۟ مِنْ خَيْرٍ
فَإِنَّ ٱللَّهَ بِهِۦ عَلِيمٌ ﴿٢٧٣﴾

> **"[Charity is] for the poor who are held back in the way of Allāh, unable to travel in the land [in search of livelihood]. The ignorant consider them wealthy because they abstain [from begging]. But you will recognise them by their [characteristic] sign, they do not ask people persistently [or at all]. And whatever good you spend on them—indeed, Allāh knows it all."**
>
> [*al-Baqarah* (2): 273]

The Prophet (ﷺ) said: "A needy person is not the one who goes from door to door, begging and is turned away with a morsel or two or with a date or two. But a needy person is the one who does not have enough to live upon, and neither from his appearance it occurs (to anyone) that he is needy and should be given charity."[171]

Some have said that they are the deprived (*maḥrūm*) as mentioned in the verse:

وَفِىٓ أَمْوَٰلِهِمْ حَقٌّ لِّلسَّآئِلِ وَٱلْمَحْرُومِ ١٩

> **"And beggars and the destitute received a due share of their wealth."**
>
> [*Al-Dhāriyāt* (51): 19]

So the Prophet (ﷺ) informed us that whoever conceals his need and it is not known whether he has more right than the one who makes his need apparent by asking, or that he has more right to charity than the other. This shows that they would not know who was in need except those that made their need apparent by asking. So a group of the scholars have differentiated between the poor

[171] Bukhārī, #1376 and Muslim, #1039 on the authority of Abū Hurayrah (*raḍiyAllāhu ʿanhu*).

(*faqīr*) and the needy (*miskīn*). They said: 'Whoever makes his need known to others then he is a *miskīn*. Whereas the one who hides his need then he is a *faqīr*.'

In the words of Imām Aḥmad there is an indication towards that, even though what is well known is that the difference is the amount of need they have or lack thereof, as is the position of many of the jurisprudents. That is to say that when the *faqīr* and *miskīn* are mentioned together as in the verse about charity. However when one is mentioned without the other then both meanings are included according to most (of the scholars).

Many of the Salaf would hide their need and would show others that they were not in need out of modesty (*ta'affaf*) and self-respect (*takkaram*). Among them was Ibrāhīm Al-Nakha'ī who use to wear fine clothes when going out while they believed he was in such need that dead meat was permissible for him.

One of the righteous would wear beautiful clothes and on his sleeve was a key to a big house while (in reality) he would have nowhere to go except the *masjid*.

Another person would not wear an outer garment in winter (to protect from the cold) due to his poverty and say: I have a problem which prevents me from wearing a padded garment when what he really meant was poverty.

Indeed the honourable is the one who conceals his hardship

Until you see him self-sufficient while in really he is making the effort (to appear as such).

This is contrary to those that would wear clothes of poor people even though they were not poor but out of humility towards Allāh, the Mighty and Majestic. In order to keep away from arrogance as was done by the four rightly guided caliphs and after them 'Umar Ibn 'Abdu'l-'Azīz. Likewise a group of the Companions, among them: 'Abdullāh Ibn 'Umar, 'Abdullāh Ibn 'Amr Ibn Al-'Āṣ and others may Allāh be pleased with all of them.

It has been narrated that Abū Bakr (*raḍiyAllāhu 'anhu*) use to say:

When you wish to be honourable among all of the people
Look at the king in the clothes of a poor man
The one whose conduct is good among the people
That is the person who is good for his worldly life and religion

'Alī (*raḍiyAllāhu 'anhu*) used to be admonished for the type clothes he dressed in, so he would say: 'It keeps one furthest away from arrogance and more worthy of a Muslim to follow me by.'[172]

'Umar Ibn 'Abdu'l-'Azīz was also reproached for the same thing, so he said: 'The best rationing is when one has the ability.' Meaning the best a person rations from his wealth is in his clothes when he has the ability to do spend.'

In the *Sunan* of Abū Dāwūd[173] and others[174] from the Prophet (ﷺ) that he said: "Shabbiness is from *īmān*" meaning austerity (*taqashuf*)."

[172] Aḥmad in his *Al-Zuhd*, p.132 and *Al-Faḍā'il*, #924 and Ḥākim, 3/143 and Abū Nu'aym in *al-Ḥilyah*, 1/82-83, and in it is Sharīk Al-Qāḍī Sadūk who is weak of memory. Reported by Aḥmad in *Al-Faḍā'il*, #923 and 'Abdullāh Ibn Aḥmad in *Zawā'id*, *Al-Zuhd*, p.131 and in *Al-Faḍā'il*, #893 and Abū Nu'aym, 1/83.

[173] Abū Dāwūd, #4161.

[174] Ibn Mājah, #4118 and others. Refer to Al-Albānī, *Silsilah al-Ṣaḥīḥah*, #341.

Reported in Tirmidhī[175] from the Prophet (ﷺ) that he said: "Whoever leaves (fine) clothes out of humility towards Allāh while he has the ability. Allāh will call him on the day of judgement (in front of all creation) until he gives him the choice of any clothes of faith he wishes to wear."

Also reported by Abū Dāwūd[176] from another chain with the wording: "Whoever leaves a beautiful garment (I think he said: *"Out of humility"*) Allāh will clothe him with clothes of honour."

What is blameworthy is when a person leaves good clothes while having the ability [the means], out of miserliness (*bukhl*). Or trying to conceal (*kitmān*) Allāh's favours (*ni'ma*) upon them. In this regard there is a well-known ḥadīth: "Indeed when Allāh gives favour to his servant He likes to see the effects of those favours upon him."[177]

So whosoever wears nice clothes showing the favour of Allāh upon himself and not out of arrogance (*ikhtiyāl*) then this is good. Many of Companions and those that came after them use to wear nice clothes such as Ibn 'Abbās (*raḍiyAllāhu 'anhumā*) and Ḥasan Al-Baṣrī.

It has been authenticated from the Prophet (ﷺ) that he was

[175] Tirmidhī, #2481 and he said: This ḥadīth is sound. Ibn Al-Jawzī said in *'Ilal*: this ḥadīth is not authentic.

[176] Abū Dāwūd, #4778. Al-Mundhirī in *Mukhtaṣar al-Sunan*, 7/164. Aḥmad in his *Musnad*, 4/438, Ṭabarānī in *al-Kabīr*, 18/281, 418. Haythamī in *Al-Majma'*, 5/132.

[177] Aḥmad in his *Musnad*, 4/438 and Ṭabarānī in *Al-Kabīr*, 18/281-418. Haythamī said in *Al-Majma'*, 5/132: Narrated by Aḥmad and Ṭabarānī and the narrators of Aḥmad are reliable.

asked about a man that likes to wear nice clothes and nice shoes? He said: "That is not from arrogance (*kibr*), rather arrogance is to rejecting the truth and looking down upon people.[178]

In other words: Arrogance (*takabbur*) is not accepting the truth (*ḥaqq*) and complying (*inqiyād*) with it, (at the same time) belittling people and holding them in contempt. This is arrogance. As for just wearing nice clothes, then it is not arrogance. Belittling people while wearing shabby clothes is arrogance.

It has also been narrated from the Prophet (ﷺ) that while he was walking there was a black female servant, so a man said to her make way for the Prophet (ﷺ)! She said: 'Let him go to the left or right.' So the Prophet (ﷺ) said: "Leave her for indeed she is arrogant." Reported by Nasā'ī[179] and others[180]

In a narration by Ṭabarānī[181] and others: They said: 'O Messenger of Allāh! Indeed she is a poor person.' He said: "That is something in her heart."

That is to say: The arrogance and pride is in her heart even though her clothes suggest she is a poor person.

[178] Muslim, #91 from the ḥadīth of Ibn Mas'ūd (*raḍiyAllāhu 'anhu*).

[179] In *Sunan Al-Kubrah*, 6/143 number, #10391 from the ḥadīth of Abū Burdah from his father. Nasā'ī said: 'Afiyah Ibn Yazīd is reliable, and I do not know Sulaymān Al-Hashimī.

[180] Abū Ya'la, #3276 and Ṭabarānī in *Al-Awsaṭ*, #8160.

[181] In *Mu'jam Al-Kabir* as in *Al-Majma'*, 1/99 from the ḥadīth of Abū Mūsā (*raḍiyAllāhu 'anhu*) with the wording: "If that is not in her power, then it is in her heart." Haythamī said: In the chain is Bilāl Ibn Abī Burdah.

Al-Ḥasan [al-Basrī] said: 'A group of people have made humbleness (*tawādi'*) in their clothes and arrogance (*kibr*) is their hearts. Some of them have more pride (*ashudu kibr*) with their outer appearance than a person who owns a bed does with his bed, or a person of the pulpit with his pulpit.'

Aḥmad Ibn Al-Hawārī said: 'Sulaymān said to me (he was like his father) what do they want from wearing wooly clothes?' I said: 'Humility (*tawādi'*).' He said: 'None of them becomes arrogance until they actually wear wooly clothes.'

Abū Sulaymān said: 'Let your outward appearance be cotton, and your inner be wool.'

Abū'l-Ḥasan Ibn Bashar said: 'Make your heart from wool, and wear fine clothes.'

So whenever a person shows his appearance as a poor person claiming righteousness (*ṣilāh*) in order to become famous among people, then that is arrogance (*kibr*) and showing off (*riyā'*). For this reason many of the sincere (*mukhliṣ*) among the Salaf avoided wearing clothes that were seen as clothes worn by the poor and righteous. And they said: 'It is glory (seeking).'

When Sayyār Abū'l-Ḥakam came to Baṣrah to visit Mālik Ibn Dinār. He wore fine clothes then entered the *masjid* and prayed. Mālik saw him (without recognising him) and said to him: 'O Shaikh! I wish to have your clothes and to pray like you.' So he replied: 'O Mālik! Do these clothes of mine lower me or raise me in status with you?'

He said: 'Rather they lower you.' So he replied: 'Yes.' The clothes may lower a person in the eyes of people, however look at your clothes (from wool) O Mālik, they may bring you down in the eyes of people but not with Allāh. So Mālik wept and stood up to embrace him. Then he asked him 'are you Sayyār Abū'l-Ḥakam?' He said: 'Yes.'

For this reason the Salaf disliked wearing clothes made from wool, such as [Imām] Ibn Sirīn and others due to the fact that it symbolized ascetic people (*zāhidūn*), clothes that make a person stand out, and make him appear to be a person of humbleness. As for the Prophet (ﷺ) he used to wear whatever he could find. So at times he would wear clothes of rich wealthy people such as the garments of Yemen or clothes of the people of Sham. Other times, he would wear clothes like the poor people which would sometimes include wooly clothes. Sometimes he would wear a cloak used when melting tar onto camels to stop certain skin conditions from spreading. As is done by the owners of camels.

Allāh did not send His Prophet (ﷺ) from the people of arrogance (*ahlul-kibr*), rather he was sent as someone who had no arrogance (*kibr*) whatsoever. Neither did he turn up his nose at jobs that people who are arrogant (*mutakabirūn*) looked down upon, such as herding camels (and sheep).

Also as a labourer for hire when the need arose for him to earn money. Whoever Allāh gave a kingdom to from them it would only increase them in submission (*tawādi'*) to Allāh, the Mighty and Majestic like [Prophet] Dāwūd (*'alayhis-salām*); [Prophet] Sulaymān (*'alayhis-salām*) and Muḥammad (ﷺ).

The word *"miskīn"* is used meaning to humble (*istikān*) one's heart to Allāh, being submissive (*tawādi'*) to His Majesty (*jalāl*); His Greatness (*'azma*); Fearing (*khashiya*) Him; Loving (*maḥabba*) Him and His Magnificence (*mahāba*).

Based on this meaning some of them have understood the following ḥadīth reported from the Prophet (ﷺ) that he said: "O Allāh let me live as a *miskīn*, let me die as a *miskīn*, and raise me up in the company of the *miskīns* (poor people)."[182] Also reported by Ibn Mājah from the ḥadīth of Ibn 'Abbās (*raḍiyAllāhu 'anhumā*).[183]

This interpretation is however not accurate because in the entire ḥadīth we find that the meaning of miskeens are the poor people, as it shows that they will they enter Paradise before the rich people. There is weakness in the both chains of narrations in this ḥadīth.

The Prophet (ﷺ) was given the choice of being a Prophet-King or a Servant-Messenger, so Jibrīl (*'alayhis-salām*) indicated to him to be more humble (*tawāḍi'*), so he (ﷺ) said: "Of course a Servant-Messenger." After that he never ate in a reclining position and said: "I eat as a servant eats. I sit as does a servant sit."[184]

[182] Tirmidhī, #2352. Tirmidhī said: This ḥadīth is strange.

[183] The author has erred in his attributing this ḥadīth to Ibn 'Abbās (*raḍiyAllāhu 'anhumā*) that was reported by Ibn Mājah. Ibn Mājah reported it on the authority of Abū Sa'īd Al-Khudrī (*raḍiyAllāhu 'anhu*), #4126. Būṣāyrī said in *Misbaḥ Al-Zujajah*: The chain of narration is weak, Abū'l-Mubārak is unknown, and Yazīd Ibn Sinān Al-Tamīmī Abū Farwah is weak.

[184] This ḥadīth has been mentioned from a number of Companions. From them:

1. 'Ā'ishah (*raḍiyAllāhu 'anhā*): Ibn Sa'īd narrated it from her in *Al-Ṭabaqāt*, 1/381, Abū Ya'lā, #492 and from Abū'l-Shaikh in *Akhlāq Al-Nabī*, p.197and Al-Baghawī in *Sharḥus-Sunnah*, #3683, and Dhahabī in *Al-Siyār*, 2/195. Haythamī said in *Majma'*, 9/19: Narrated by Abū Ya'lā and its chain is good. Dhahabī said in *Al-Siyār*, 2/195: This ḥadīth is ḥasan gharīb.
2. Anas (*raḍiyAllāhu 'anhu*): Narrated from him by Ibn Shahīn in *Nasikh Al-Ḥadīth wa'l-Mansūkh*, #637.
3. Ibn 'Abbās (*raḍiyAllāhu 'anhumā*). Narrated by Nasā'ī from him in

Al-Ḥasan said: 'The Prophet (ﷺ) said: "Allāh gave me for making that (choice), (the gift of) being made the leader of all the sons of Adam. The first one to intercede and the first to have his intercession accepted. The first to have the earth open up above (to

al-Kubrā, #6743 and Bukhārī in *Tārikh Al-Kabir*, 1/124, and Ṭabarānī in *Al-Majma'*, 9/20: In the chain is Baqiyah Ibn Walīd and he is a Mudallis. I said: In the chain is a break between Muḥammad Ibn 'Alī Ibn 'Abdullāh Ibn 'Abbās and his grandfather Ibn 'Abbās. Al-'Irāqī declared this ḥadīth weak in *Takhrīj al-Iḥyā'*, 3/340. He narrated the ḥadīth mursal from Zuhrī and Ta'ūs and Yaḥyā Ibn Abi Kathīr and Al-Ḥasan. As for the Mursal of Zuhrī it is reported by Ma'mmar in his collection, #19551. As for the Mursal of Ta'ūs then it is also reported by Ma'mmar, #19552. As for the Mursal of Yaḥyā Ibn Abī Kathīr then it was reported by Ma'mmar too, #19554, and via him Bayhaqī in *Shu'ab*, #5975. Ibn Sa'd in *Al-Ṭabaqāt*, 1/371. Al-Ḥāfiẓ said in *Talkhīs Al-Ḥabīr*, 3/125 after mentioning the ḥadīth, and Abū'l-Shaikh in *Akhlāq Al-Nabī* from the ḥadīth of Jābir (*raḍiyAllāhu 'anhu*), and from 'A'ishah (*raḍiyAllāhu 'anhā*) and the chains are weak. Also Ibn Shahīn through 'Atā' Ibn Yassār in Mursal (missing the name of the Companion in the chain) form. Then he mentioned the narration of 'Ā'ishah (*raḍiyAllāhu 'anhā*) that is with Ibn Sa'd, and said: Bayhaqī has said in *Al-Shu'ab* and *Dalā'il* from the ḥadīth of Ibn 'Abbās (*raḍiyAllāhu 'anhumā*) in a story about which he said: The Prophet (ﷺ) did not eat after that any food while reclining until he met Allāh (until his death). Narrated by Nasā'ī with the wording: *"At all"* instead of "Until he met Allāh". The chain is good from the narration of the others from Zubaydī and he clearly stated it, and was agreed with by Mu'ammar from Zuhrī and also reported by 'Abdu'l-Razzāq. 'Ajlūnī mentioned in *Kashf Al-Khufā'*, 1/17: The ḥadīth: "I eat as a slave eats, and I sit as a slave sits." He said: Ibn Sa'd narrated it with a good chain and Abū Ya'la on the authority of 'Ā'ishah (*raḍiyAllāhu 'anhā*). In a narration of Al-Bayhaqī from Yaḥyā Ibn Abī Kathīr in mursal form with the addition: Indeed I am a slave. Narrated by Ḥannād in *Al-Zuhd*, #800 from 'Amr Ibn Murra also in Mursal form with the wording: I eat as a slave eats, so by the one whose hand my soul is in if the world was weighed with Allāh the weight of a wing of a gnat He would never give a single vessel of drink to a disbeliever.

Each part of this ḥadīth has support which makes it stronger.

be resurrected)." It has also been authenticated from him that he (ﷺ) said: "Indeed I am a servant, so say: ' Servant of Allāh and His Messenger.'[185] The most noble of names are 'Abdullāh (servant of Allāh) so for this reason this name is used for the Prophet (ﷺ) in the best of places in the Qur'ān. When he (ﷺ) established servitude (*'ubudiyya*) to his Lord, he obtained leadership over all of creation.

Many of the knowledgeable people (*'ārifin*) use to say in their conversations with Allāh: 'It is enough of a reason for me to have pride (*fakr*) that I am Your servant (*'abd*), and sufficient for me as an honour (*sharf*) that you are my Lord (*Rabb*).'

Whenever I remember that He is my Lord and I am his servant, it gives me such joy (*surūr*) that my body cannot contain.

The honour of souls is entering into servitude
While the slave embraces pride with his possessor

Abū Yazīd Al-Basṭāmī use to chant:

O if only I became something
From nothing to being of worth
I have become master over all
Because I am your slave.

So whoever submits his heart (*qalb*) to Allāh, the Most High, and is fearful (*khashiya*), showing humility (*tawādi'*), Allāh will aid him and raise him accordingly. In the well-known narration: Allāh said to [Prophet] Mūsā (*'alayhis-salām*) while he asked him: 'Where can I find you?' He said: 'With those whose hearts are broken because

[185] Bukhārī, #3445 on the authority of 'Umar Ibn Al-Khaṭṭāb (*raḍiyAllāhu 'anhu*).

of me, indeed I draw closer to them every day by a hand span. If I didn't then they would be destroyed.'[186]

'Abdullāh Ibn Salām (*raḍiyAllāhu 'anhu*) said while explaining: 'They are hearts submitted to the love of Allāh away from love of others besides Him.'

In a famous narration (allegedly) from the Prophet (ﷺ) [in which it is claimed he (ﷺ) said]: "Indeed, Allāh, the Most High when he manifests himself to His creation it fears Him. So when the greatness of Allāh, His Majesty and Magnificence is revealed to the hearts of those that have awareness, they lower themselves out of awe for Him, having fear and submitting to Him out of love and fear."[187]

The poorest of people even love their graves
It is merely dust of humility in among the graveyards

The *miskīn* in reality is the one who lowers (*istikān*) his heart to his Lord, he fears Him from his piety (*khashiya*) and loves (*maḥabba*) Him. The *miskīn* can not be worthy of praised except those who have this description. Whoever's heart does not have fear of Allāh in spite of his poverty and need then he is arrogant (*faqr*). Like that black servant that the Prophet (ﷺ) said about: "Indeed she is arrogant (*jabāra*)."

[186] Ibn Abī 'Āṣim in *Al-Zuhd*, 1/57 and Abū Nu'aym in *al-Ḥilyah*, 6/177 from 'Imrān Al-Qasīr who said: Mūsā said, in it is a break between 'Imrān and Mūsā (*'alayhis-salām*). Reported by Abū Nu'aym in *al-Ḥilyah*, 2/364 from Mālik Ibn Dinār who said: Mūsā (*'alayhis-salām*) said also has a break in the chain. Al-Qarī said in *Al-Asrar Al-Marfū'ah*, p.118: It has no basis.

[187] Note: I have not found this ḥadīth and I think it is most likely fabricated.

So he is either destitute (*'ā'il*) and arrogant (*mutakabbir*), or poor (*faqīr*) and self-conceited (*mukhtāl*). Both types of people Allāh will not look at on the Day of Judgment. The believer submits his heart to Allāh and is submissive, showing his humility and poverty during times of hardship and prosperity (*rikhā'*). So while being in a pleasing state (*riḍā*) he shows gratitude (*shukr*), and during times of hardship he shows humility (*dhull*), servitude (*'ubudiyya*), insufficiency (*faqā*) and his need (*ḥajā*) until he is relieved of the hardship (*kashf al-darr*). Allāh, the Most High says:

وَلَقَدْ أَخَذْنَٰهُم بِٱلْعَذَابِ فَمَا ٱسْتَكَانُوا۟ لِرَبِّهِمْ
وَمَا يَتَضَرَّعُونَ ﴿٧٦﴾

"Indeed, We seized them with the punishment, but they did not humble themselves before their Lord nor will they invoke (Allāh) with submission to Him ."

[*Al-Mu'minūn* (23): 76]

So He rebuked those that did not submit themselves to their Lord during their times of hardship. When Prophet (ﷺ) used to come out seeking rain (*istisqā'*), he would do so with humility, fearful of His Lord and would be dressed in a dishevelled way.[188]

Mutrif Ibn 'Abdullāh was detained by a relative of his so he wore two worn out garments, and then took hold of a stick and said: 'I show humility to my lord so that he may intercede for me because of it.'

It has been legislated to show this state of humility to Allāh dur-

[188] Aḥmad in his *Musnad*, 1/230, Abū Dāwūd, #1165, and Tirmidhī, #558, #559 and he said: It is ḥasan ṣaḥīḥ. Also Nasā'ī, 3/156-157, and Ibn Mājah, #1266.

ing the prayer as in the ḥadīth of Al-Faḍl Ibn 'Abbās (*raḍiyAllāhu 'anhuma*) from the Prophet (ﷺ) who said: "The Prayer is two (units), make *tashahhud* after every two units. Have fear, humility and be in the state of submissiveness to your Lord. Show your need by raising your hands and saying: 'O my Lord,' three times. Whoever does not do so then it (the prayer) is aborted."'[189] Reported by Tirmidhī[190] and others.[191]

Also it is legislated to show this state of humility in supplications.

Ṭabarānī reported[192] from the ḥadīth of Ibn 'Abbās (*raḍiyAllāhu 'anhuma*) who said: 'I saw the Prophet (ﷺ) supplicate in 'Arafat with his hands to his chest like how a poor person asks for food.'

Also from his ḥadīth[193] is what the Prophet (ﷺ) said in his supplication during the last part of 'Arafat: "I am the humble poor person, seeking your aid and assistance. The one who has fear and is caring. The one who acknowledges his sins and like the one who is frightened. I ask you like the poor people, I beseech

[189] In the Imbrosiana manuscript: This phrase *"three times"* has reoccurred, and in the *Sunan* of Tirmidhī: then it is such and such.

[190] Tirmidhī, #385 and reported the statement of Bukhārī: and the ḥadīth of Layth Ibn Sa'd is authentic, meaning it is more authentic than that of Shu'bah.

[191] Aḥmad in his *Musnad*, 1/211 and Nasā'ī in *Al-Kubra* and in *Tuhfaḥ Al-Ashrāf*, 8/264 and Abū Dāwūd, #1296 and Nasā'ī in *Al-Kubra* as in *Tuhfaḥ Al-Ashrāf*, 8/391 and Ibn Mājah, #1325.

[192] In *Al-Awsaṭ*, #2892 on the authority of Ibn 'Abbās (*raḍiyAllāhu 'anhumā*). Haythamī said in *Al-Majma'*, 1/168: In the chain is Al-Ḥusayn Ibn 'Abdullāh Ibn Ubaydullāh, and he is weak.

[193] Part of a ḥadīth reported by Ṭabarānī in *Al-Kabīr*, 11/11495 and *Al-Ṣaghīr*,

you like the sinful and humble person. I invoke you like the scared blind person."

One of the Salaf used to sit at night with his head lowered [bent] down and stretching his hands in silence like a poor beggar. Tāūs said: "Alī Ibn Al-Ḥusayn Al-Ḥajr entered his room one night and prayed. I heard him say in his prostration: 'I am your slave whom you can cause to perish, your poor person whom you can cause to perish, your needy person whom you can cause to perish and your beggar whom you can cause to perish.'

Ṭāūs said: 'I memorised these words, and I did not invoke those words in any calamity (*karb*) except that it was removed from me.'

One of the worshippers made *ḥajj* eighty times by foot. While he was doing tawaf he was saying: 'O my beloved.' He heard a voice saying: 'Are you not be pleased to be a *miskīn* (needy person), until you become a beloved person.' He went into a daze, after that he started to say: '(I am) your *miskīn*, (I am) your *miskīn*.'

Shaikh al-Islām Ibn Taymiyyah (may Allāh have mercy upon him) said:

I am in dire need of Allāh, the Lord of the heavens
I am weak in every aspect my life
I am oppressive to myself and it oppresses me
All goodness that comes to me is from Him

= 1/247 and Al-Khaṭīb in *Tarīkh*, 6/163 from the same chain also: Ibn Al-Jawzī in *'Ilal*, #1412 on the authority of Ibn 'Abbās (*raḍiyAllāhu 'anhumā*). Haythamī said in *Al-Majma'*, 3/252: In the chain is Yaḥyā Ibn Ṣāliḥ Al-Iblī, Al-'Uqailī said: Yaḥyā Ibn Bakīr has narrated from him rejected narrations; the other narrators are of Bukhārī. Ibn Al-Jawzī said: The ḥadīth his not authentic. Al-'Irāqī said in *Takhrīj ul-Iḥyā'*, 1/254: The chain is weak.

The statement of Prophet (ﷺ):

« وأن تغفر لي وترحمني »

"and that you forgive me and have mercy on me."

Forgiveness (*maghfira*) and mercy (*raḥma*) bring together all of the good (*khayr*) of the Hereafter. This is because forgiveness covers sin along with saving you from the evil consequences. It has been said: Forgiveness does not come together with evil consequences, and for this reason *mighfar* (cloth worn on the head) is named as such to cover the head and save it from harm. This is the opposite to the word *"Afu'* (pardon) which means it may sometimes come before the punishment or after.

As for mercy, then it is to enter Paradise and reach the highest of ranks (*'ulu darajāt*). Along with all the bliss (*na'īm*) [or blessings] that is therein from what is created. From the pleasure of Allāh is, being close (*qurb*) to Him, looking (*mushāda*) at Him and visiting Him is from the mercy of Allāh. In an authentic ḥadīth (it is mentioned): 'Indeed Allāh the Mighty and Majestic says to Paradise: "You are my mercy, by you I show mercy to whomsoever of my servants I wish."'[194]

Everything that is in Paradise is from His [the Mighty and Majestic] mercy. His mercy cannot be achieved through action alone as he (ﷺ) said:[195] "Your actions alone will not save any of you."

[194] The reference for this has preceded.

[195] Bukhārī, #6467 and Muslim, #2818 on the authority of 'Ā'ishah (*raḍiyAllāhu 'anhā*). Also Reported by Bukhārī, #6423 and Muslim, #2816 on the authority of Abū Hurayrah (*raḍiyAllāhu 'anhu*). See the detail explanation of this ḥadīth published under the title, *'The Journey to Allāh'* by Imām Ibn Rajab published by Dār as-Sunnah Publisher, Birmingham, U.K, 2007, 1st ed.

They asked: 'Messenger of Allāh, not even you?'
He replied : "Not even me, unless Allāh were to envelop me in His mercy."

His statement (ﷺ): "When you wish a calamity to befall a people to take my life without being put to trial." The meaning behind this supplication (*du'ā'*) is the safety of the servant (*salāma al-'abd*) from the trials of this world (*fitna al-dunyā*) as long as one lives. For if Allāh decrees a trial he takes His servant back to Himself (i.e. causes his death) before that trial occurs. This is from the most important of supplications (*ahamm al-ad'iyyah*). Indeed the believer who lives his life free of any trials then Allāh takes his life before they occur and the people fall into them, then this is his salvation (*najā*) from all evil (*sharr*). The Prophet (ﷺ) ordered his Companion to seek refuge in Allāh from trials that are both apparent (*ẓahr*) and hidden (*baṭin*).[196]

In another ḥadīth:

«وجنِّبنا الفواحش والفتن ما ظهر منها وما بطن»

> "Keep us away from rudeness and trials that are open and hidden."[197]

He used to single out specific trials by name. He used to seek refuge in his prayer from four things and he used to order others also to seek refuge in these four trails:

[196] Part of a ḥadīth reported by Muslim, #2867 on the authority of Zayd Ibn Thābit (*raḍiyAllāhu 'anhu*) in elongated form.

[197] Part of a ḥadīth reported by Abū Dāwūd, #969, and Ibn Mājah, #2429, and Ḥākim, 1/265 and he said: Authentic according to the criteria of Muslim.

«أعوذ بالله من عذاب جهنم، ومن عذاب القبر، ومن فتنة المحيا والممات، ومن فتنة المسيح الدجّال»

> "I seek refuge in the punishment of the hell (*jahannam*) fire, from the punishment of the grave (*qabr*), from the trial of life and death (*fitna al-maḥyā wa'l-mamāt*) and from the trial of the false messiah (*masiḥ al-dajjāl*).[198]

'Trial of life' includes trials of both religion and the world, such as disbelief (*kufr*) [in another manuscript—poverty (*faqr*)], innovations (*bid'ah*) flagrant sins (*fusuq*) and disobedience (*'isyān*). Trial of death includes a bad ending (*su' al-khatima*) to a person's life and the trial of the two angels in the grave (*fitna al-mālikayn fi'l-qabr*). Indeed the people will be put to test in their graves similar to or close to the trial of the anti-Christ.

Then he mentioned the trial of the anti-Christ due to its importance, because there will be no trial before the Day of Judgment greater than the anti-Christ. As the time draws closer to the last hour trials will increase.

In the ḥadīth of Mu'āwiyyah (*raḍiyAllāhu 'anhu*) from the Prophet (ﷺ) who said: "There will remain nothing in the world except adversity (*balā'*) and trials (*fitnah*)."[199]

The Prophet (ﷺ) informed us of the trails that will come like

[198] Bukhārī, #833 and Muslim, #589 on the authority of 'Ā'ishah (*raḍiyAllāhu 'anhā*). Reported by Muslim, #588 on the authority of Abū Hurayrah (*raḍiyAllāhu 'anhu*) and Ibn 'Abbās (*raḍiyAllāhu 'anhumā*), #590 with various wordings.

[199] Aḥmad, (4/94), and Ibn Mājah, #4035 and Būṣāyrī said in *Al-Zawā'id*: The chain is authentic and the narrators are reliable.

parts of a dark night, and man will wake up a believer (mu'min) but by evening he will be a disbeliever (*kāfir*), selling his religion for some trivial worldly gain."[200]

The first trial to appear is what happened after the reign 'Umar (*raḍiyAllāhu 'anhu*), the killing of 'Uthmān (*raḍiyAllāhu 'anhu*). Along with the consequences that followed from the spilling of blood, the hearts were divided and innovations appeared in the religion. Such as the innovation of Khawārij apostates of the religion and what they gave rise to. Then the appearance of innovations from the people of *Qadr* (Qadarīyah and Jabarīyyah) and Rāfiḍah (Shi-ite) etc. These trials came like waves in an ocean as mentioned in the famous ḥadīth of Hudayfah (*raḍiyAllāhu 'anhu*) when he was asked by 'Umar (*raḍiyAllāhu 'anhu*).[201] Hudayfah (*raḍiyAllāhu 'anhu*) use to ask the most questions to the Prophet (ﷺ) about trials out of fear of falling into them.[202] When he came close to dying he said: 'A beloved (death) has come (to me), upon poverty (*faqā'*). The one with regret (*nadm*) will not prosper. All praise be to Allāh that has made me die before the trial, whose leaders are from the disbelievers (from the non-Arabs).'[203]

His death was before the murder of 'Uthmān (*raḍiyAllāhu 'anhu*) by forty days. Others have said: 'Rather his death came after the murder of 'Uthmān.'

In those days a man from the Companions was asleep, when a man came to him in his sleep and said to him: 'Stand up! And ask

[200] Muslim, #118 on the authority of Abū Hurayrah (*raḍiyAllāhu 'anhu*).

[201] Bukhārī, #7096, and Muslim, #144.

[202] Bukhārī, #7084, and Muslim, #1847.

[203] Abū Nu'aym in *Al-Ḥilyah*, 1/282.

Allāh to give you refuge from the trial that His righteous servants have sought refuge from. So he stood up, made ablution, prayed, then he beseeched Allāh and died shortly after.'

It has been narrated from the Prophet (ﷺ) that he said to a man: "When I, Abū Bakr, 'Umar and 'Uthmān die, if you are able to also die then do so."[204]

This is an indication of these trials which occurred with the murder of 'Uthmān (*raḍiyAllāhu 'anhu*).

To supplicate for death out of fear of trials in the religion is permissible. The Companions and the righteous after them used to do so. When 'Umar (*raḍiyAllāhu 'anhu*) made his last pilgrimage he lay down on a flat piece of land then he raised his hands and said:

---

[204] Reported by Al-'Uqaylī in *Ḍhu'afa*, 2/165-166, and Ibn 'Adī in *Al-Kāmil*, 4/351. Ibn Ḥibbān in *Al-Majruḥīn*, 1/341 from Salim Ibn Maymūn Al-Khawāṣ who narrated to Sulaymān Ibn Ḥayyān who narrated to me Ismā'īl Ibn Abī Khālid from Qais from Sahl Ibn Abī Ḥathmahthmah. Then he mentioned the ḥadīth.

Al-'Uqailī said concerning Salm: He narrated rejected ḥadīth that are not followed and he mentioned this ḥadīth as an example.

Ibn Ḥibbān said about him: He was from the worshippers of *Sham* and reciters from those that righteousness overwhelmed him until he neglected the memorising of ḥadīth and being precise in it. So maybe he mentioned something after something else and then turned it around in confusion not deliberately, so he is not to be used as proof unless other reliable narrators agree with what he said.

Ibn 'Adī said about him: he narrated from a group of reliable narrators but they did not follow him in what he narrated his text and chains of narrations. Then he mentioned this ḥadīth and said: Salm Al-Khawāṣ has narrations, and this ḥadīth he did not narrate from Sulaymān Ibn Ḥayyān other than Salm Al-Khawāṣ, and he has other narrations other than what I have mentioned with known chains and texts. He is counted from the major Ṣūfis, and ḥadīth was not from his actions. Maybe he intended to be right but made a mistake in the narration and text, because it was not from his practice.

اللهم إنّـه قد كـبرت سِنِّي، ورقّ عَظْمي،
وانتشرت رعيتي، فاقبضني إليك غيرَ مُضَيِّع ولا مفتون.

> "O Allāh I have become old in age, my bones are weak, my rule has spread far and wide so take my life without me being abandoned nor put to trial."

Then he returned to Madīnah and a month did not pass before he was killed. May Allāh have mercy upon him.'[205]

'Alī supplicated to his Lord when he became weary of people he was ruling and shortly after he was also killed. Zainab Bint Jahsh (*raḍiyAllāhu 'anhā*), supplicated when a gift of wealth came from 'Umar (*raḍiyAllāhu 'anhu*) and she found it was too much, she said: 'O Allāh let not another gift from 'Umar reach me after this one. She died shortly before the next one came.'[206]

When 'Umar Ibn 'Abdu'l-'Azīz became tired with his flock (the people who he ruled over) due to the weight of him establishing the truth over them and trying to fulfil their rights. So he called upon a man who was known for his supplications to be accepted and asked him to supplicate to Allāh for death for him. The man supplicated for 'Umar Ibn 'Abdu'l-'Azīz and himself, they both died soon after. A group of the pious Salaf were called to take control of the judiciary, so they sought a three day respite. Then they supplicated to Allāh for death and they died shortly after.

The good deeds of one of the righteous Salaf were discovered, even though he kept it a secret (*sirr*) between himself and his Lord.

---

[205] Mālik in *Muwaṭṭa*, 2/824 and Abū Nu'aym in *al-Ḥilyah*, 1/53.

[206] Ibn Sa'd in *al-Ṭabaqāt*, 3/300-301, 8/109-110, and Abū Nu'aym in *al-Ḥilyah*, 2/54.

So when he became aware that his good actions were exposed, he asked Allāh to take his soul out of fear (*kawf*) of the trial of fame and he died shortly after.

Indeed fame in relation to good deeds is a trial, as is mentioned in the ḥadīth: "It is enough for a person as a trial that people point to him with their fingers (out of fame), indeed it is a trial."[207]

Sufyān Al-Thawrī use to wish for death frequently so he was

---

[207] Ṭabarānī in *Al-Kabīr*, 8/210-228, and Al-'Uqaylī in *Ḍhu'afa*, 4/7 and from the same chain Ibn Al-Jawzī in *Al-'Ilal*, #1380 and Abū Nu'aym in *al-Ḥilyah*, 5/247. Also Bayhaqī in *Shu'ab*, #6979 on the authority of 'Imrān Ibn Ḥusayn (*raḍiyAllāhu 'anhu*) directly from the Prophet (ﷺ): 'It is sufficient a sin for a person that he be pointed out with (other people's) fingers.' They said: 'O Messenger of Allāh even if it is for something good?' He said: 'If it is for good then it is just flattery except who Allāh has mercy upon, and if is for something evil then it is evil.'

Ibn Al-Jawzī said: It is not authentic. It was declared weak by Al-'Irāqī in his checking of *Al-Iḥyā'*, 3/276. Reported by Al-Bayhaqī in *Shu'ab*, #6977 from the ḥadīth of Anas (*raḍiyAllāhu 'anhu*) directly from the Prophet (ﷺ): "Sufficient evil for a person, except who Allāh protects, that people point to him with their fingers because of his worldly or religious (condition)." Munāwī said in *Al-Fayḍ*, 3/197: In the chain is Yūsuf Ibn Ya'qūb. If he was the Naysabūrī then Abū'l- 'Alī Al-Ḥāfiẓ said: I have not seen a person in Naysabūr who lies besides him. And if he is the judge from Yemen then he is unknown and Ibn Lahi'ah his weakness has been mentioned previously.

Al-Bayhaqī from 'Atā' Al-Khurasanī on the authority of Abū Hurayrah (*raḍiyAllāhu 'anhu*) with this wording. In the chain is Kalthūm Ibn Muḥammad Ibn Abī Sidrah. Abū Ḥātim said: They speak about. (*Al-Lisān*, 4/489) and 'Atā' did not hear from Abū Hurayrah (*raḍiyAllāhu 'anhu*) and therefore the chain is broken. (*Jāmi' Al-Tahsīl* page 290-291). Also reported by Ṭabarānī in *Al-Awsaṭ* (*Majma' Al-Bahrain*: *Qaf* 496) from another chain by Abū Hurayrah (*raḍiyAllāhu 'anhu*). Al-Haythamī said; (10/297): In the chain is 'Abdu'l-'Azīz Ibn Ḥusayn and he is weak. Bayhaqi indicated that chain, and said: This chain is weak. And the ḥadīth was declared weak by Al-'Irāqī in *Takhrīj al-Iḥyā'*, 3/275. I said: Al-Ḥasan has used the word *"an 'an"* instead of stating clearly he heard it.

asked about it, to which he said: 'I don't know if I might fall into innovation, or perhaps fall into something not permissible, or fall into trial, so if I die then I would have preceded all of that. Know that a person is never free from trial.'

Ibn Mas'ūd (*raḍiyAllāhu 'anhu*) said: 'Let not any one of you say:

اعوذ بالله من الفتن،

'I seek refuge in Allāh from trials (*fitan*)',

rather say:

أعوذ بـالله من مُضِلّاتِ الفتن.

'I seek refuge from trials that lead one astray (*muḍalāt al-fitan*).'

Then he read the statement of the Most High:

إِنَّمَآ أَمۡوَٰلُكُمۡ وَأَوۡلَٰدُكُمۡ فِتۡنَةٞۚ

"Your wealth and your children are only a trial."
[*al-Taghābun* (64): 15]

He is referring to the fact that wealth and children should not be sought refuge from as they are trials. In the *Musnad* it is reported that Prophet (ﷺ) ordered Umm Salāmah (*raḍiyAllāhu 'anhu*) to say:

«اللهم رب النبي محمد اغفر لي ذنبي، وأذهب غيظ قلبي،
وأجرني من مضلات الفتن ما أبقيتني»

"O Allāh, Lord of Prophet Muḥammad forgive me my

[208] Part of a ḥadīth reported by Aḥmad, 6/301-302, on the authority of Umm Salamah (*raḍiyAllāhu 'anhā*). Haythamī, 7/211, said: In the chain is Shahr, who has been declared reliable and has a weakness. He also said, 10/176: The chain is ḥasan.

sins, take away the rancour that is in my heart and save me from the trials that lead one astray as long as you keep me (alive)."[208]

The Prophet (ﷺ) defined women and wealth as a trial. In the Ṣaḥīḥ of Bukhārī the Prophet (ﷺ) said: "I have not left behind a trial more harmful (*adar*) to the men than women (*nisā'*)."[209]

Also reported in Bukhārī[210] from the Prophet (ﷺ): "By Allāh, it is not poverty (*faqr*) that I fear for you. Rather I fear that the world will open up to you, as it opened up to those before you. You will compete with each other for it, as they did, and it will destroy you as it destroyed them."

Reported in the Ṣaḥīḥ of Muslim[211] from the Prophet (ﷺ) who said: "Fear women, for indeed the first trial of the children of Israel was women."

Likewise, reported in Tirmidhī[212] that the Prophet (ﷺ) said: "Every nation has a (main) trial, and the trial of my nation is wealth (*māl*)."

Allāh, the Mighty and Majestic says:

[209] Bukhārī, #2740, and Muslim, #2740 on the authority of Usamah Ibn Zayd (*raḍiyAllāhu 'anhu*).

[210] Bukhārī, #3158, and Muslim, #2961 on the authority of 'Amr Ibn 'Awf (*raḍiyAllāhu 'anhu*).

[211] Muslim, #2742 on the authority of Abū Sa'īd Al-Khudrī (*raḍiyAllāhu 'anhu*).

[212] Tirmidhī, #2336 and Tirmidhī said: ḥasan gharīb

وَجَعَلْنَا بَعْضَكُمْ
لِبَعْضٍ فِتْنَةً أَتَصْبِرُونَ ۗ وَكَانَ رَبُّكَ بَصِيرًا ﴿٢٠﴾

"And We have made some of you [people] a trial for others— to see if you will have patience? Your Lord Sees everything."

[*al-Furqān* (25): 20]

So the man is a trial for the woman and the woman a trial for the man. The wealthy are a trial for the poor, and the poor are a trial for the wealthy. The sinful person is a trial for the righteous person, and the righteous is a trial for the sinful person. The disbeliever is a trial for the believer, and the believer is a trial for the disbeliever. Allāh says:

وَكَذَٰلِكَ فَتَنَّا بَعْضَهُم بِبَعْضٍ لِّيَقُولُوٓا۟ أَهَٰٓؤُلَآءِ مَنَّ ٱللَّهُ
عَلَيْهِم مِّنۢ بَيْنِنَآ ۗ أَلَيْسَ ٱللَّهُ بِأَعْلَمَ بِٱلشَّٰكِرِينَ ﴿٥٣﴾

"In this way We have tried some of them by means of others so that they might say, 'Are these the one's whom Allāh has bestowed His favour upon amongst us?' Does not Allāh know best as to who are thankful [to Him]?"

[*al-An'ām* (6): 53]

And He says:

وَنَبْلُوكُم بِٱلشَّرِّ وَٱلْخَيْرِ فِتْنَةً ۖ وَإِلَيْنَا تُرْجَعُونَ ﴿٣٥﴾

"And We test you with both evil and with good by way of trial. And to Us you all will be returned."

[*Anbiyā'* (21): 35]

So He made all that befalls a person from good or bad a trial. That is to say, it is a trail that one is tested by. So when they are given good their gratitude is tested, and when evil befalls them their patience is tested.

The trial of prosperity and ease is more difficult to bear than that of adversity. 'Abdu'l-Raḥmān Ibn 'Awf (*raḍiyAllāhu 'anhu*) said: 'We were tested with the trial of adversity (*darrā'*) [in the time of the Messenger (ﷺ)] and we were patient. When we were tested with the trial of prosperity (*sarrā'*) we were not patient.'[213]

One of them said: 'The trial of adversity is something that the sinful (*fājir*) and righteous person (*barr*) can bear with patience (*ṣabr*). But the trial of prosperity can only be endured with patience by the truthful (*ṣiddīq*).'

When Imām Aḥmad was afflicted with the trial of adversity [of whether the Qur'ān was a created thing, while the correct belief is that the Qur'ān is the Speech of Allāh and not created] he was patient and was not restless, he said: 'It increased me in my faith.' However when he was tested with the trial of ease he became restless, he wished for death day and night fearing that it was a deficiency in his religion.

Indeed the believer will be put to test with something of trials that are difficult and full of hardship so that their faith (*īmān*) is tested as Allāh, the Most High says:

الٓمٓ ﴿١﴾ أَحَسِبَ ٱلنَّاسُ أَن يُتْرَكُوٓا۟ أَن يَقُولُوٓا۟ ءَامَنَّا وَهُمْ لَا
يُفْتَنُونَ ﴿٢﴾ وَلَقَدْ فَتَنَّا ٱلَّذِينَ مِن قَبْلِهِمْ ۖ فَلَيَعْلَمَنَّ ٱللَّهُ ٱلَّذِينَ
صَدَقُوا۟ وَلَيَعْلَمَنَّ ٱلْكَـٰذِبِينَ ﴿٣﴾

"Alif, Laam, Meem. Do the people think that they

[213] Reported by Ibn Al-Mubārak in *al-Zuhd*, #519, and Tirmidhī, #2464 and he said it is ḥasan, and Abū Nu'aym in *al-Ḥilyah*, 1/100.

will be left alone (at ease) because they say, 'We believe' and they will not be tested? We have certainly tested those lived before them, and Allāh will surely make evident those who are truthful, and He will surely make evident the liars."

[*al-'Ankabūt* (29): 1-3]

However Allāh is kind to His believing servants in these trials, He gives them patience and He rewards them. He does not throw them into trials that lead to misguidance or destruction which take away their religion. Rather these trials come to them while they are in a state of good health.

Ibn Abī Al-Dunya reported from the ḥadīth of Ibn 'Umar (*raḍiyAllāhu 'anhumā*) directly from the Prophet (ﷺ): "Indeed Allāh has special people from His servants, they live their life in Allāh's mercy, He keeps them in good health, and take them into His Paradise. They are the ones that trials come to them as parts of the night, while they will be saved from it."[214]

The minor trials that a person is tested with regarding his family, wealth, children and neighbour can be expiated through acts of obedience (*ṭā'āt*) such as prayer (*ṣalāh*), fasting (*ṣiyām*) and charity (*ṣadaqah*). This is what is mentioned in the ḥadīth of Hudayfah (*raḍiyAllāhu 'anhu*).[215]

[214] Ṭabarānī in *Al-Kabīr*, 12/13425 and in *Al-Awsaṭ*, #6369, and Al-'Uqailī, 4/152. Also Abū Nu'aym in *Al-Ḥilyah*, 1/6 on the authority of Ibn 'Umar (*raḍiyAllāhu 'anhumā*), and in the chain is Muslim Ibn 'Abdullāh (about whom) Al-'Uqailī said: He is unknown in narrating and his narrations are not preserved. And he said: Narrations in this subject are subject to flexibility. Al-Dhahabī said in *al-Mīzān*, 4/105: It is not known, and the information is rejected. Haythamī, 10/266, said: In the chain is Muslim Ibn 'Abdullāh Al-Humasī and I do not know him. Al-Dhahabī declared him unknown, and the other narrators he declared reliable.

[215] The checking has preceded.

It is narrated by Hudayfah (*raḍiyAllāhu 'anhu*) that he asked the Prophet (ﷺ) [by saying]: "Indeed my tongue has a sharpness, and most of it is (used) upon my family. So he replied: "Where you are with seeking forgiveness (*istighfār*)?"[216]

As for the trials that lead one astray [from the straight path], the trails which corruption (*fisād*) [in the religion] is feared from, are the ones which refuge should be sought from. Death should be asked for before such trials occur. Whoever dies before the trials befall the people, Allāh has preserved and protected him.

In the *Musnad* from Maḥmūd Ibn Labīd (*raḍiyAllāhu 'anhu*) from the Prophet (ﷺ) who said: "Two things are disliked by the son of Adam: he hates death, but death for the believer is better than the trials. He hates having less wealth, and less wealth means less to answer for [on the Day of Judgement]."[217]

The statement of the Prophet (ﷺ):

(وأسألك حُبَّك، وحُبَّ من يُحِبُّك، وحُبَّ العمل الذي يُبلِّغني حبَّك).

> "I ask you for your love and the love of the one who loves you and love of those actions that will draw me closer to your love."

[216] Aḥmad in his *Musnad*, 5/394,396, 397, 402, and Dārimī, 2/302. Also Nasā'ī in *'Aml al-Yawm wa'l-Layl*, 338-353 and Ibn Mājah, #3817 on the authority of Hudayfah (*raḍiyAllāhu 'anhu*). Būṣāyrī said in *Al-Zawā'id*: In the chain Abū'l-Mughirah Al-Bajalī defective in ḥadīth from Hudayfah (*raḍiyAllāhu 'anhu*). Al-Dhahabī said so in *Al-Kashif*.

[217] Aḥmad in his *Musnad*, 5/427, 428, and Al-Baghawī in *Sharḥ Al-Sunnah*, 14/267 on the authority of Maḥmūd Ibn Labīd (*raḍiyAllāhu 'anhu*). Haythamī said in *Majma'*, 10/257: Aḥmad narrated it with two chains, one of which is used as evidence in Bukhārī.

This supplication (*du'ā'*) gathers all good (*khayr*). Indeed all the chosen actions of the servant come from love and the ability to to do good. So if the love of Allāh is firm in the servant 's heart then the movements that come from his limbs are according to what Allāh loves and is pleased with. Hence the servant loves all those actions and speech which is loved by Allāh. The love of Allāh will lead a servant to do good and leave all evil actions. And He loves those from His creation, that love Him.

This supplication was invoked by the Prophets (*'alayhis-salām*) as in Tirmidhī[218] that the Prophet (ﷺ) said: 'That Dāwūd (*'alayhis-salām*) used to say:

اللهم إني أسألك حبَّك، وحبَّ من يحبك، وحبَّ عمل يبلِّغُني إلى
حبَّك، اللهم اجعل حبَّك أحبَّ إليَّ من نفسي وأهلي ومن الماء البارد»

> "O Allāh, I ask you for your love, the love of those who love you, and to love those deeds that will bring me closer to your love. O Allāh, make your love more beloved to me than myself, my family and even cold water."'

Also [reported in Tirmidhī][219] is that the Prophet (ﷺ) used to supplicate:

«اللهم ارزقني حبَّك، وحبَّ من يحبُّك،
وحُبَّ عمل يبلِّغُني إلى حبِّك، اللهم ما رزقتني مما أحبُّ فاجعله قوةً لي فيما
تحبُّ، وما زَويت عني مما أحب فاجعله فراغاً لي فيما تحبُّ»

> "O Allāh, bless me with your love, the love of those that

---

[218] Tirmidhī, #3490 and Tirmidhī said: This ḥadīth is ḥasan gharīb. Sh. Albani has declared it weak.

[219] Tirmidhī, #3491 and Tirmidhī said: This ḥadīth is ḥasan gharīb. Sh. Albani has declared it weak.

> love you, the love of those actions that will bring me closer to your love. O Allāh,Whatever you have given from things that I love, make it a source of strength for me to gain your love, and whatever you remove from me from things that I love, then replace it with something you love."

In a mursal ḥadīth, it has been reported by Ibn Abī Al-Dunya and others that the Prophet (ﷺ) used to say:

(اللهم اجعل
حبّك أحبَّ الأشياء إليّ ، وخشيتَك أخوفَ الأشياء عندي ، واقطع عني حاجات الدنيا بالشوق إلى لقائك ، وإذا أقررت أعينَ أهل الدنيا من دنياهم فأقرر عيني من عبادتك)

> "O Allāh make your love the most beloved thing to me, your fear the most feared thing to me, cut off my needs [or desire] of the world with eagerness to meet you. When the eyes of the people of the world are cooled by things from this world, make my eyes cool with your worship."[220]

Whoever is only concerned with seeking the love of Allāh, then Allāh will give him above what he needs from the world as a result. One of the Salaf said: 'When Dāwūd (*'alayhis-salām*) died, Allāh sent (a Messenger) to Sulaymān (asking him): 'Do you have a need that you want to ask me?' Sulaymān replied: 'I ask Allāh that He make my heart love Him the same as my father Dāwūd use to love Him. And that He makes my heart fear Him as the heart of my father Dāwūd use to fear Him.' So Allāh was pleased with him and gave him a kingdom that He gave to nobody else besides him.'

[220] Abū Nu'aym in *Al-Ḥilyah*, 8/282 from Al-Haytham Ibn Mālik Al-Ṭā'ī in mursal form.

The Love of Allāh is of two levels:

One of them is: Obligatory (*wājib*). This love brings about for the servant the love of all that Allāh loves from the obligatory actions (*wājibāt*). And to hate all those forbidden actions (*muḥaramāt*) that He hates. Indeed complete love (*al-muḥabbah al-tām*) necessitates agreement (for the one that is loved, or beloved) in loving whatever he loves, and hating (*karāha*) whatever he hates, especially in those things that the one loving, loves and hates himself. So love is not valid if it is without doing what the beloved (*maḥbūb*) wants from the one who loves him, and hates what the beloved hates from the one who loves him.

One of those who had knowledge was asked about love, to which he replied: Agreement in all instances. He then chanted:

If you said to me die, I would die out of hearing and obeying
And I would say to the caller of death welcome

Another person said:

You disobey Allāh while you claim love of Him
Then this, is by my life, a heinous comparison
Indeed the one who loves is obedient to his beloved

So whenever a servant fails to meet some of the obligations, or falls into some of the forbidden actions, then his love for his Lord is incomplete. He must rush to repent (*tawbah*), and strive hard to perfect his love which will lead him to perform all the obligatory actions and avoid all forbidden acts. This is the meaning of the statement of the Prophet (ﷺ): "A fornicator does not fornicate while he is a believer, nor does a thief steal while he is a believer. A person does not drink alcohol while he is believer." [221]

[221] Bukhārī, #2475 and Muslim, #57 on the authority of Abū Hurayrah (*raḍiyAllāhu 'anhu*).

Indeed complete faith (*al-īmān al-kāmil*) necessitates loving that which Allāh loves, and hating what He hates, along with doing the actions that go with (having that love). So no one falls into any of the forbidden actions or falls short in any of the obligations except that he has put forward his own desires (*hawā*) over the love of Allāh, the Most High, which would make him do the opposite of that.

The second level of love: The level of those that are close (*darajah al-muqarribīn*). This is to have the heart filled with love to the point that it makes the person love even the optional actions (*maḥabbah al-nawāfil*), and striving (*ijtihād*) to perform them. Hating the forbidden things and staying well away from them. Being pleased with the things that have been predestined (*riḍa bi'l-qadiyya*) which cause pain to the souls, because they have come from the one who is beloved. As 'Amir Ibn Qais said: 'I loved Allāh to the point where any affliction that befell me was made light, He pleased me with every trial. So I don't care because of my love for Him, in which state I enter upon the morning or evening.'

'Amir Umar Ibn 'Abdul-'Azīz said after his pious father had died: 'Indeed Allāh loved for him to be taken, and I seek refuge in having love for something which opposes the love of Allāh.'

He used to say: 'When I woke up in the morning, I find no other happiness (*surūr*) except in places that predestination (*qaḍā'*) and pre-decree (*qadr*) have occurred.'

Some of them chanted:

O the one whose separation we find most difficult
Our hearts are no more after you
if your happiness is in what I'm afflicted with

Then what are wounds when pain is what pleases you
In line with control of the heart
To find sweetness in all that brings pain

'Ammār Ibn Yāsir (*raḍiyAllāhu 'anhu*) used to say: 'O Allāh if I knew that it was most pleasing to you that I throw myself from this mountain and tumble down then I would have done it. If I knew that it was pleasing to you that I light a large fire and then fall into it I would have done so. If I knew that it was pleasing to you that I throw myself into the water and drown I would have done it. Indeed I only say this out of desire for your face. I hope you will not prevent me from your face while that is all I seek.'[222]

One of the righteous Salaf's two sons were killed in the way of Allāh, so people came to pay their condolences so he cried and said: 'I do not weep because of their loss, rather I weep (wondering) how their (effort in) pleasing Allāh was at the time when the swords took them.'

One of the knowledgeable people was going around the Ka'bah when the Qaramita (Shite sect) attacked the people killing many in their wake whilst they were going around the Ka'bah. When they reached this knowledgeable person he did not stop doing what he was doing until he fell down from the blows of their swords so he said:

You see those that have love falling down in their homes
Like the youth of the cave who did not know
how long they remained
The least price a person with love can pay is with his soul:
With the blood of the loving one he sells to reach them

---

[222] Abū Nu'aym in *Al-Ḥilyah*, 1/142-143 on the authority of 'Ammār (*raḍiyAllāhu 'anhu*) with similar wording.

So who is there that will pay the price

One of the knowledgeable people said: 'Either you are ready to sell your soul (*rūḥ*) in this way, or you do not busy yourself with falsehood.'

Take a chance with your soul in our love and then take rest
If you wish to lay claim to a greater place
Do not be distracted from reaching us
Stand up on the foot of hope and send forth

As the love of Allāh, the Mighty and Majestic has prerequisites (*lawāzam*), which is love that which Allāh loves from people and their actions and hating what He hates. The Prophet (ﷺ) asked Allāh with his love for Allāh and love of two more things.

[6.1. Love that which Allāh Loves]

Firstly: Love that which Allāh, the Most High loves. So whoever loves Allāh, loves those that Allāh loves and ally themselves to them. Hating His enemies and those that show enmity to them as the Prophet (ﷺ) said: "Three attributes that if they are found in someone will have the sweetness of faith (*ḥalāwa al-īmān*): That Allāh and His Messenger are more beloved to him than everybody else, and that a person only loves for the sake of Allāh....the rest of the ḥadīth."[223]

The ones deserving to be loved the most for Allāh, are His Prophets and Messengers. His greatest Prophet (ﷺ) is Muḥammad, the one whom Allāh has ordered His creation to follow. He also

[223] Bukhārī, #16 and Muslim, #43 on the authority of Abū Hurayrah (*raḍiyAllāhu 'anhu*).

made following him a sign of the truthfulness of their love for Him. As Allāh, the Most High says:

قُلْ إِن كُنتُمْ تُحِبُّونَ ٱللَّهَ
فَٱتَّبِعُونِى يُحْبِبْكُمُ ٱللَّهُ وَيَغْفِرْ لَكُمْ ذُنُوبَكُمْ ۗ وَٱللَّهُ غَفُورٌ رَّحِيمٌ

"Say, [O Muḥammad], 'If you love Allāh, then follow me, [so] Allāh will love you and forgive you your sins. Allāh is Ever-Forgiving, Most Merciful.'"

[*Āl-'Imrān* (3): 31]

And He has warned in the following verse those who give precedence to the love of something He created over loving Him, loving His Messenger, and loving to strive in His path (*sabīl*):

قُلْ إِن
كَانَ ءَابَآؤُكُمْ وَأَبْنَآؤُكُمْ وَإِخْوَٰنُكُمْ وَأَزْوَٰجُكُمْ وَعَشِيرَتُكُمْ
وَأَمْوَٰلٌ ٱقْتَرَفْتُمُوهَا وَتِجَٰرَةٌ تَخْشَوْنَ كَسَادَهَا وَمَسَٰكِنُ
تَرْضَوْنَهَآ أَحَبَّ إِلَيْكُم مِّنَ ٱللَّهِ وَرَسُولِهِۦ وَجِهَادٍ
فِى سَبِيلِهِۦ فَتَرَبَّصُوا۟ حَتَّىٰ يَأْتِىَ ٱللَّهُ بِأَمْرِهِۦ ۗ وَٱللَّهُ لَا يَهْدِى
ٱلْقَوْمَ ٱلْفَٰسِقِينَ ﴿٢٤﴾

"Say, [O Muḥammad], 'If your fathers or your sons or your brothers or your wives or your relatives or any wealth which you have obtained, or any business you fear may slump, or any house which pleases you, are more beloved to you than Allāh and His Messenger and striving in His cause, then wait until Allāh brings about His command. Allāh does not guide people who are deviators.'"

[*al-Tawbah* (9): 24]

He described those who have love for Him as being gentle with the believers: by having compassion; mercy and love for them.

And being firm towards those who do not believe: by detesting [their disbelief] and striving in the way of Allāh. He, the Most High, says:

يَٰٓأَيُّهَا
ٱلَّذِينَ ءَامَنُواْ مَن يَرۡتَدَّ مِنكُمۡ عَن دِينِهِۦ فَسَوۡفَ يَأۡتِي ٱللَّهُ بِقَوۡمٖ يُحِبُّهُمۡ
وَيُحِبُّونَهُۥٓ أَذِلَّةٍ عَلَى ٱلۡمُؤۡمِنِينَ أَعِزَّةٍ عَلَى ٱلۡكَٰفِرِينَ يُجَٰهِدُونَ فِي
سَبِيلِ ٱللَّهِ وَلَا يَخَافُونَ لَوۡمَةَ لَآئِمٖۚ ذَٰلِكَ فَضۡلُ ٱللَّهِ يُؤۡتِيهِ مَن يَشَآءُۚ
وَٱللَّهُ وَٰسِعٌ عَلِيمٌ ٥٤

"O you who have believed! if any of you renounce your religion—Allāh will bring forth [in place of you] a people He will love and who will love Him, [who are] humble toward the believers, stern to the unbelievers, who strive in the way of Allāh and do not fear the blame of any critic. That is the unbounded favour of Allāh, which He bestows it upon whom He wills. And Allāh is All-Encompassing and All-Knowing."

[*Al-Mā'idah* (5): 54]

[6.2. Love those Actions which Allāh Loves]

Secondly: The love of what Allāh, the Most High, loves of those actions that will draw you closer to reach His love. Here there is an indication that the level of Allāh's love is reached only through acts of obedience and those things that He loves. So when a servant implements the commands of Allāh their Protector, and does what Allāh, the Most High, loves, He raises him to the level of His love as in the ḥadīth qudsi collected by Bukhārī: "My servant does not get closer to me in a way better than performing what I have made obligatory upon him. My servant continues to get closer to me by doing optional good deeds, until I love him."[224]

The best actions that bring about the love of Allāh is by doing the obligatory deeds (*fi'l-wājibāt*), and leaving bad deeds (*tark al-muḥaramāt*). For this reason the Prophet (ﷺ) made a sign of finding sweetness of faith (*ḥalāwa al-īmān*) to hate to return to disbelief (*kufr*) as a person would hate to be thrown into the fire.

Dhūn-Nūn was asked: 'When will I love my Lord?'
He said: 'When what He hates is more distasteful to you than patience (*ṣabr*).'

Then after that to strive in doing the optional good deeds (*nawāfil*), and leaving those small issues that are disliked or not clear.

From the greatest of optional good deeds to obtain the love of Allāh is reading the Qur'ān (*tilāwa*), especially with contemplation (*tadbīr*). Ibn Mas'ūd (*raḍiyAllāhu 'anhu*) said: 'No one should ask about themselves, except that they use the Qur'ān to evaluate themselves with. Whoever loves the Qur'ān then he loves Allāh and His Messenger.'

This is why the Prophet (ﷺ) said to the one who said he loved *Surah Ikhlāṣ* because it was a description of the Most Merciful: "Inform him that Allāh loves him."[225]

---

[224] Bukhārī, #6502 on the authority of Abū Hurayrah (*raḍiyAllāhu 'anhu*).

[225] Bukhārī, #7375, and Muslim, #813 on the authority of 'Ā'ishah (*raḍiyAllāhu 'anhā*).

Abū Salāmah Ibn 'Abdu'l-Raḥmān said: 'When the Prophet (ﷺ) came to Madīnah he gave a sermon and in it he said: "Indeed the best speech is the speech of Allāh, successful is he who Allāh beautifies with the Qur'ān in his heart, enters into Islām after disbelief, and He chose it (the Qur'ān) over all other speech. Indeed it is the best of speech and most eloquent. Love whomever Allāh loves and love Allāh with all your heart."[226]

One of them used to read the Qur'ān abundantly and then became tired from doing so. He then saw in a dream someone saying to him:

If you claim to love me
Why have you deserted my book
Have you not pondered?
Over my kind reproach
He soon woke up and returned to reading

[6.3. Actions that help You reach the Love of Allāh]

Among the actions that help us reach the love of Allāh the Most High, and it is among the greatest signs of those that love (*muḥibbūn*):

Always remembering Allāh (*dhikr*), the Mighty and Majestic, in the heart (*qalb*) and on the tongue (*lisān*).

One of them said: 'No one is addicted to the remembrance of Allāh except that he benefits by achieving the love of Allāh.'

---

[226] Bayhaqī in *Dalāil Al-Nabuwah*, 2/524-525 on the authority of Abū Salamah Ibn 'Abdu'l-Raḥmān in Mursal form.

Dhūn-Nūn said: 'Whoever is accustomed to remembering Allāh, Allāh will ignite in his heart a flame which will make him yearn to (meet) Allāh.'

One of the Companions of the Prophet's (ﷺ) said: 'The sign of the love of Allāh is excessive remembrance of Him, for indeed you do not love anything except you remember it a lot.'

Fatḥ Al-Mousalī said: 'The one who loves Allāh does not find in the world any pleasure (*ladha*), nor does he forget to remember Allāh for even a blink of an eye (*tarfa 'ayn*).

So those that have this love when they speak, speak with remembrance of Allāh (*dhikr*), and when they are silent are busy with reflection (*fikr*).

If I speak I will not do so without mentioning You
And in my silence You are still the cause

[6.4. Love of being Alone to Converse with Allāh]

Among the signs of those that love Allāh, and it is something also that will help obtain the love of Allāh, is love of being alone to converse (*ḥubb al-khalwa*) with Allāh, the Most High, especially during the night:

The night is for me and for my loved ones
I will talk to them [at night]
So let me talk to them at our times of gathering

Fuḍayl said: Allāh, the Mighty and Majestic says: 'Those that claim to love me have lied, if when night time falls they are sleep. Does not everyone who loves someone want to be alone with them? Here I am watching my beloved, when the night falls upon them, they put their eyes in their hearts and I present myself in front of them.'

So address me in view of me, and speak to me in my presence, tomorrow I will make the eyes of those that love me cool in my gardens.

Your eyes sleep and (yet) you complain of (lack of) affection
If you were in love, you would not be asleep

The hearts of those that love are like stones under the darkness of the night, every time the gentle wind of early morning bustles it bursts into flames.

The passing of the gentle breeze reminds me of your love
I increase in yearning each time it passes me by
I see myself each time the night comes lit up
By lamps with the fire of passion in my heart

As the night time comes in the one who has love starts to yearn:

If only you were to see the people of affection
When the stars appear
Here someone lamenting their sins
Another praying and bowing

So the one who does not have their piety will not comprehend what makes them weep, in the same way whoever did not witness the beauty of Yusuf does not understand the pain Ya'qūb felt in his heart. Al-Sirī Al-Saqtī said about his condition:

Whoever sleeps while his heart is being squeezed
Cannot then realize (the feeling) of his insides crumbling

Where are the men of the night?
Where are (the likes of) Ibn Adham and Fuḍayl?

The heroes have gone and the idle remain. You who are pleased with just the appearance of being humble, or just being poor in name, or wearing wool as your only means of showing humility, and from praising (Allāh) just beads.

Where is the virtue of Fuḍayl?
Where is the striving of Junayd?
Or the secret of Sirī?
Or the joy of Bishr?
Or the zeal of Ibn Adham?

Woe unto you if you're not able to know what is good then lament those gone forth.

Here lie there empty fields where they used to be
All withered away so accuse what destroyed them
I called out while in my heart there was fire
O place when did your people leave you

O you who has change of heart! You who had time with Allāh then it went away, standing (*qiyām*) in the early hours is longing for you. Fasting (*ṣiyām*) during the day is asking about you. The nights rebuke you for cutting them off from them:

Have you become busy with others away from us?
Showing abandonment this is not how we use to be
You swore not to change your love
You have freed yourself from a life of love while we haven't
Nights we take from your fruits
My heart yearns for those nights (to return)

My brothers, the gatherings of remembrance (*majālis al-dhikr*) are the drink of those people of love (*sharāb al-muḥibīn*) and an antidote for those that have sinned:

قَدْ عَلِمَ كُلُّ أُنَاسٍ مَّشْرَبَهُمْ

"Each (group of) people knew its own watering place."

[*al-Baqarah* (2): 60]

The gatherings of remembrance end sorrow, so someone weeps over his sins, another due to his faults, another regretful still for missing what he sought, while another grieving the rejection of his beloved, someone announcing his passion, while another still bewailing his loss (or distance from it).

I don't reminisce our life that has passed by
Except that the heart has become faded and deserted
Woe be to days gone by that were pure
How sorrowful, and will my sorrow bring what is lost?
Only if we were at the water of Zamzam and the black stone
O our amazement just before the last days of pilgrimage
Will the best days of my life return
I know what I wished for I did not know

As if I see those accepted being taken away. As if I can see angels greeting those who repent, come let us weep over the rejected:

Time ceases not to be exposed for pleasure
As long as it turns away from us
Time evaded us and did not find
A substitute besides us so you wept over past times
If you had stayed standing by our door

You would have worn from our kindness and removed pleasure
Instead you left our rights and abandoned us
So the world grew narrow in spite of its great expanse

The book is now complete.
All praise and ability to do good belongs to Allāh,
peace and blessings be upon our Leader Muḥammad,
and his Family and Companions.

www.ingramcontent.com/pod-product-compliance
Lightning Source LLC
Chambersburg PA
CBHW051902090426
42811CB00003B/436
9781643544168